Jeff N

Developing, Assessing, ar   ....g inquiry-Based
Instruction

Jeff Marshall & Robert Horton

Developing, Assessing, and Sustaining Inquiry-Based Instruction

A Guide for Math and Science Teachers and Leaders

VDM Verlag Dr. Müller

Impressum/Imprint (nur für Deutschland/ only for Germany)

Bibliografische Information der Deutschen Nationalbibliothek: Die Deutsche Nationalbibliothek verzeichnet diese Publikation in der Deutschen Nationalbibliografie; detaillierte bibliografische Daten sind im Internet über http://dnb.d-nb.de abrufbar.
Alle in diesem Buch genannten Marken und Produktnamen unterliegen warenzeichen-, marken- oder patentrechtlichem Schutz bzw. sind Warenzeichen oder eingetragene Warenzeichen der jeweiligen Inhaber. Die Wiedergabe von Marken, Produktnamen, Gebrauchsnamen, Handelsnamen, Warenbezeichnungen u.s.w. in diesem Werk berechtigt auch ohne besondere Kennzeichnung nicht zu der Annahme, dass solche Namen im Sinne der Warenzeichen- und Markenschutzgesetzgebung als frei zu betrachten wären und daher von jedermann benutzt werden dürften.

Coverbild: www.purestockx.com

Verlag: VDM Verlag Dr. Müller Aktiengesellschaft & Co. KG
Dudweiler Landstr. 99, 66123 Saarbrücken, Deutschland
Telefon +49 681 9100-698, Telefax +49 681 9100-988, Email: info@vdm-verlag.de

Herstellung in Deutschland:
Schaltungsdienst Lange o.H.G., Berlin
Books on Demand GmbH, Norderstedt
Reha GmbH, Saarbrücken
Amazon Distribution GmbH, Leipzig
ISBN: 978-3-639-17847-0

Imprint (only for USA, GB)

Bibliographic information published by the Deutsche Nationalbibliothek: The Deutsche Nationalbibliothek lists this publication in the Deutsche Nationalbibliografie; detailed bibliographic data are available in the Internet at http://dnb.d-nb.de.
Any brand names and product names mentioned in this book are subject to trademark, brand or patent protection and are trademarks or registered trademarks of their respective holders. The use of brand names, product names, common names, trade names, product descriptions etc. even without a particular marking in this works is in no way to be construed to mean that such names may be regarded as unrestricted in respect of trademark and brand protection legislation and could thus be used by anyone.

Cover image: www.purestockx.com

Publisher:
VDM Verlag Dr. Müller Aktiengesellschaft & Co. KG
Dudweiler Landstr. 99, 66123 Saarbrücken, Germany
Phone +49 681 9100-698, Fax +49 681 9100-988, Email: info@vdm-verlag.de

Copyright © 2009 by the author and VDM Verlag Dr. Müller Aktiengesellschaft & Co. KG and licensors
All rights reserved. Saarbrücken 2009

Printed in the U.S.A.
Printed in the U.K. by (see last page)
ISBN: 978-3-639-17847-0

ACKNOWLEDGEMENTS

We owe a debt of gratitude to many. From the students who inspire us to the teachers and educational leaders who challenge us to help improve teaching and learning, we thank you for your participation, involvement, and insights. It is with great appreciation that we thank the teachers and administrators from Greenville and Oconee County School Districts in South Carolina. The conversations, observations, and interactions contributed significantly to the contents within this book.

Many individuals have played a key role in the development of the efforts that follow. Julie Smart has worked tirelessly with us for three years in researching, writing, editing, and facilitating interactions with the schools. Ben Sloop has contributed greatly to the data collection and classroom observations for the project, and he has also given us valuable assistance in research and editing. Cathy Plowden, whose work is described in Chapter 7, provided a setting that allowed us to see how students responded to many of the ideas discussed in this book.

The research efforts of this book were supported by the Inquiry in Motion Institute and Clemson University's Center of Excellence for Inquiry in Mathematics and Science (CEIMS). Funding for the Institute and the Center have been provided by the South Carolina Commission on Higher Education, Clemson University, and Greenville County Schools.

Finally, we would like to thank the many people who have reviewed various chapters of the book. These individuals include the following former students, current teachers, colleagues, and educational leaders: Kathy Howard, Diane Ricciardi, Cathy Plowden, Tammie Mirolli, Jordan Rapp, and Vicki Phillips. The expertise and perspective that these educators have given us have been invaluable.

TABLE OF CONTENTS

INTRODUCTION

In recent decades, many commissions, researchers, and organizations have called for improved learning in mathematics and science[1-6]. Some of these calls are based on a need for economic competitiveness[7,8], while others are broader, calling for schools to better develop critical thinking skills in all students. Whatever the motivation, inquiry-based instruction can be a powerful method for both improved learning and the development of critical thinking.

The calls for reform have led to much debate about how to define mathematics and science, what students should know and be able to do, and how we should best prepare our students for the world of tomorrow. Many of the arguments are based on a false dichotomy that separates learning content from developing proficiency in the scientific process. We believe that content and process are both critical and best achieved in tandem. Specifically, learning that promotes deep understanding of content is achieved when we actively engage students in meaningful inquiry that is targeted at important concepts in mathematics and science[4,6,9-11].

The idea of inquiry-based instruction is not new, nor is it the latest educational fad to hit the professional development circuits. It has been around since before Dewey and has been shown to be effective at helping students go beyond the superficial, rote memorization that is soon forgotten, which is so prevalent in classrooms today[12-14]. Although the fundamental principles have been with us for decades, we have made great strides in understanding inquiry-based instruction and in creating tools and instruments that can help teachers use inquiry more effectively. In this book, we present several innovations that are designed to help teachers improve the quality of inquiry in their own classrooms.

INQUIRY CLARIFIED

Since this book encourages and supports the development of inquiry-based practices in math and science classrooms, it is important to be clear on what we mean by inquiry-based instruction. Many definitions of inquiry-based instruction exist. Most involve describing a student-centered approach in which students explore ideas and think critically about the content. We have adopted a definition from the science standards:

Inquiry-based instruction refers to the development of understanding through investigation, i.e., asking questions, determining appropriate methods, gathering data, thinking critically about relationships between evidence and explanations, and formulating and communicating logical arguments—adapted from the National Science Education Standards, 1996, p. 105.

For us, the key facet is that students must explore the concepts before receiving or developing their own explanation. When we begin with the abstract ideas for which students do not have prior experiences or knowledge, they are forced to memorize rather than understand at deeper levels. Effective inquiry, along with other constructivist approaches, has students connect concepts and ideas to their own experiences. This enables them to make more sense of the content, gaining ownership of the ideas so that they are more likely to retain knowledge and transfer it to new situations.

ISSUES IN MATH AND SCIENCE

Having students explore concepts before moving on to the underlying abstract ideas is a fundamental principle of inquiry that is common for all disciplines. This seemingly simple principle is at the core of our work and this book. When teachers get students truly engaged exploring the concepts in contexts where meaning exists, students develop both a need and a desire to know and to learn.

Despite this crucial connection, the content domains of math and science are far from identical. Perhaps the most significant difference is that most branches of mathematics carry the burden of proof, whereas science contends that there is a tentative nature to results that can change based on new data. In our view, however, this fundamental difference between the disciplines is not as pronounced as it first might appear. While science may not be able to claim absolute "proof," students still seek to provide sufficient support and justification for their conclusions. In both disciplines, students should formulate hypotheses, gather evidence, reason from data, draw conclusions, and then provide substantial justification for these conclusions. In mathematics, the burden of proof can hinder learning when students are expected to prove theorems without sufficient prior experiences with the content. Proving ideas has merit, but it is where in the instructional sequence that these ideas are proved that must change. Our inquiry lessons should culminate with proofs rather than be initiated with them.

Another area of difference between mathematics and science is the vocabulary we use, beginning with the word "inquiry" itself. Though prominent in science, this word is not nearly so prevalent in mathematics education. "Problem solving" and "problem-based learning" are two expressions, among others, that are more frequently used in the mathematics education literature. However, the focus on problem solving is not in and of itself complete enough for guiding the process of learning entailed in inquiry-based learning. Problem solving has been a focus for NCTM since the 1980 "Agenda for Action,"[15] but it is only one of five key processes identified by the national math standards[4], which also include connections, mathematical reasoning, communication, and representation. When all five of these processes are united with content-based objectives then effective inquiry-based instruction is achieved. Stated differently, these five processes serve both as goals (e.g., we want our students to be able to reason mathematically) and as a means toward learning rich standards-based content. With this understanding, inquiry becomes a more powerful approach to facilitate learning.

OVERVIEW OF CHAPTERS

This book lays out what we have developed over the last few years to help teachers be more effective as they develop, implement, and assess inquiry-based instruction. The discussion in Chapter 1 is framed by the results from a survey we conducted of more than 1200 math and science teachers. These teachers, on average, reported using inquiry almost 40% of their instructional time and wished, on average, to increase it by almost another 20%[16]. We were surprised by their perceptions of their current practice and excited about the ideals that they possessed for where they would like their practice to be. Meaningful professional development supported by initiatives such as the one described in this book provides an excellent venue to encourage teachers to achieve their reported ideals. Further, based on our subsequent work, we have found that professional development opportunities can help improve the quality of inquiry instruction being led.

Chapter 2 focuses on a clear framework to guide teachers as they facilitate inquiry instruction. Engaging students in activities by itself does not constitute inquiry, at least not how we are defining it. Further, we do not view inquiry-based instruction as free discovery, but rather as an intentional, instructional method that guides students as they engage their prior knowledge, explore a particular concept by gathering and analyzing data, explain what they have seen as they develop the underlying ideas, and then extend these ideas to different contexts as they deepen their understanding. The target is always in mind—internalizing and mastering the standards, which, of course, have already been identified by our professional organizations. The 4E x 2 Instructional Model discussed in Chapter 2 originates from considerable research regarding developing and implementing inquiry-based lessons[14]. The Model integrates formative assessment and reflective practice into each of the key stages of inquiry.

Chapter 3 applies the Model by providing an overview and tutorial of a Dynamic Web Tool that supports teachers as they plan and implement inquiry instruction. Since planning is often very time consuming, especially for newer teachers, the Web Tool provides a resource for teachers to implement previously created lessons, modify existing lessons, create new lessons, and interact with other professionals.

Chapter 4 helps teachers and educational leaders determine what inquiry is and what it is not. Over three years of research and validation, we developed the Electronic Quality of Inquiry Protocol (EQUIP) to assess the quality of inquiry in the classroom[17,18]. EQUIP provides descriptive rubrics on 19 indicators associated with effective inquiry-based instruction. By using EQUIP, we can move from making unsubstantiated claims about the quality of inquiry being facilitated to assessing what is actually occurring in the classroom. This offers a means of providing both an assessment of where things currently stand and a vision of where we want to go.

In Chapter 5, we discuss how to determine whether inquiry-based practices or other initiatives actually have a positive impact upon student achievement. Despite all of the tests that our students take, high-stakes and otherwise, it is still difficult to determine whether teachers and programs have the effect that we want on students' learning. Consequently, we thought it important for the reader to see how this might be accomplished and how we determine the impact our own work with teachers has upon student achievement.

Chapter 6 focuses on classroom management issues, which are the source of great fear and frustration for teachers in both inquiry and non-inquiry settings. In this chapter, we provide suggestions and guidelines that we hope give readers sufficient information to allay their fears and move toward practice with a greater emphasis upon inquiry.

Then, in Chapter 7, we suggest a strategy for how to establish a plan to improve the quality of inquiry in the class. Included is a discussion of some of the challenges that teachers face when shifting from a traditional method to an inquiry-based method.

To take firm root, any major initiative must have support from educational leaders. Chapter 8 provides suggestions for these leaders, for they play a crucial role in supporting a transformation to inquiry-based practices, yet have often not had the opportunity to stay current in best practices in mathematics and science.

The change to an inquiry-based approach is not easy. It requires a great deal of thought and effort and often asks more from teachers than traditional approaches do. We believe, however, that this shift is well worth the effort. The evidence suggests that inquiry-based instruction, which is advocated by leaders in both math and science education, can improve student achievement in your school and better prepare students at all academic levels and abilities to think critically, solve problems, and learn content. We hope that this book provides the information and support that you seek as you, your department, your school, or your district moves toward high-quality sustained inquiry-based practice. Please let us know how we can continue to best help in this regard.

ENDNOTES

1.   American Association for the Advancement of Science, *Science for all Americans*. Oxford University Press: New York, 1990.

2.   National Commission on Excellence in Education *A nation at risk: An imperative for educational reform*; US Department of Education: Washington, DC, 1983.

3.   National Commission on Mathematics and Science Teaching, *Before its too late: A report to the nation from the National Commission on Mathematics and Science Teaching for the 21st Century*. U.S. Department of Education: Washington, DC, 2000.

4.   National Council of Teachers of Mathematics, *Principles and standards for school mathematics*. NCTM, Inc.: Reston, VA, 2000.

5.   National Research Council, *National science education standards*. National Academies Press: Washington, DC, 1996.

6.   National Research Council, *Inquiry and the national science education standards: A guide for teaching and learning*. National Academies Press: Washington, DC, 2000.

7.   Friedman, T., *The world is flat: A brief history of the twenty-first century*. Farrar, Straus and Giroux: New York, 2005.

8.   National Academy of Sciences, *Rising above the gathering storm: Energizing and employing America for a brighter economic future*. National Academies Press: Washington, DC, 2007.

9.   American Association for the Advancement of Science, *Blueprints for reform*. Oxford University Press: New York, 1998.

10.   American Association for the Advancement of Science, *Atlas of science literacy: Project 2061*. AAAS & NSTA: Washington, DC, 2001.

11.   National Board for Professional Teaching Standards, *What teachers should know and be able to do*. Author: Washington, DC, 1994.

12.   Bybee, R. W.; Taylor, J. A.; Gardner, A.; Scotter, P. V.; Powell, J. C.; Westbrook, A.; Landes, N. *The BSCS 5E instructional model: Origins, effectiveness, and applications*; BSCS: Colorado Springs, June-July, 2006; p 49.

13.   Llewellyn, D., *Teaching high school science through inquiry: a case study approach*. NSTA Press & Corwin Press: Thousand Oaks, CA, 2005.

14.   Marshall, J. C.; Horton, B.; Smart, J., 4E x 2 Instructional Model: Uniting three learning constructs to improve praxis in science and mathematics classrooms. *Journal of Science Teacher Education* In Press.

15.   National Council of Teachers of Mathematics, *An agenda for action: Recommendations for school mathematics of the 1980s.* NCTM: Reston, VA, 1980.

16.   Marshall, J. C.; Horton, B.; Igo, B. L.; Switzer, D. M., K-12 science and mathematics teachers' beliefs about and use of inquiry in the classroom *International Journal of Science and Mathematics Education* 2009, 7, (3), 575-596.

17.   Marshall, J. C.; Horton, B.; White, C., EQUIPping teachers: A protocol to guide and improve inquiry-based instruction. *The Science Teacher* 2009, 76, (4), 46-53.

18.   Marshall, J. C.; Smart, J.; Horton, R. M., The Design and Validation of EQUIP: An Instrument to Assess Inquiry-Based Instruction. *International Journal of Science and Mathematics Education* In Press.

CHAPTER 1

THE CURRENT STATE OF INQUIRY-BASED INSTRUCTION

Our experiences coupled with existing research have provided convincing evidence that inquiry-based instruction has a positive, significant impact upon student achievement in mathematics and science. Consequently, our work over the last few years has been designed to help teachers construct and implement inquiry-based practices in their own classrooms. One of the things that we have learned is that, in order for significant conceptual change to occur, we must first engage the prior knowledge of the learner[1-3]. Without engaging this prior knowledge, learning is mostly superficial and quickly forgotten. The same must hold true for teachers as they look to improve their instructional practice. Their learning must also build upon their prior experiences and understandings before a shift to inquiry-based instruction can be achieved successfully. Therefore, before we offered professional development experiences designed to improve teachers' classroom practice, we found it important to first understand their perceptions and beliefs regarding inquiry-based instruction.

To do so, we began by working with Greenville County School District (GCSD), one of the nation's largest school districts (over 68,000 students) and the largest in South Carolina. GCSD serves a diverse urban, suburban, and rural student population. As a means to gain an understanding of the current state of inquiry-based instruction and to establish some baseline data, we conducted a survey of the mathematics and science teachers in the district. More than 60% of the district's K-12 math and science teachers (n = 1,222) responded to the survey.

Inquiry-based instruction is a complex, multifaceted method, and successful implementation is based on numerous factors. We chose, based on research, to explore the teachers' perceptions of their behaviors, beliefs, and motivations in regard to inquiry-based instruction. Teachers' perceptions are quite important; for example, if they believe that they are doing something (e.g., facilitating inquiry learning 40% of the time), then this perception guides their reflection on their teaching, interactions with students, and curricular decisions. However, if their perceptions do not match what is observed during their instruction, then any discrepancies must be addressed before practice will likely change.

Further, if teachers' belief structures and motivation are not sufficient to support a transition to inquiry-based instruction, then we should address these explicitly in some meaningful way. One course of action involves getting teachers to discuss barriers and work collaboratively to resolve them. Closely related is the issue of support: if teachers are motivated to do something, in this case lead inquiry-based instruction, then they are more likely to do so if the proper support mechanisms are in place to encourage them.

Our findings from this study provided the impetus for our subsequent work with teachers and our own research. Specifically, math and science teachers collectively reported spending on average 39% of their time on inquiry-based instruction. Although this is obviously a significant amount, teachers on average wished to increase this by almost 20%. This led to two significant goals of our professional development work with the teachers in the district. First, because the teachers reported spending such a significant amount of time on inquiry, we wanted to assess the quality, so we determined that we needed a reliable and valuable method to help us achieve this assessment. Second, once we could assess the quality of inquiry, we set out to increase both the quantity and the quality of inquiry that was occurring in the classroom.

Before we delve into the details of these two goals, we discuss in greater detail the current state of inquiry instruction as viewed by the teachers in our targeted school district. We believe that this large, diverse district is representative of many school systems throughout the nation. However, we leave it to you to determine how well our results align with your own personal experiences and views. With kind permission of Springer Science and Business Media, the following is a reprint and adaptation of an article published in the *International Journal of Science and Mathematics Education* by Marshall, Horton, Igo, and Switzer[4]. As you read it, we suggest that you consider the following:

1) How well do the teachers' views of the percent of time they *typically* use for inquiry-based instruction and the *ideal* percent of time they should spend on inquiry-based instruction align with your views?

2) To what extent do you believe your school leaders, peers, and curriculum support inquiry-based practices?

3) How confident are you in your ability to implement inquiry-based practices effectively?

4) Do you have the content and pedagogical knowledge essential to lead inquiry-based instruction effectively?

INTRODUCTION

The goal of providing high-quality science and mathematics instruction in the K-12 classroom remains elusive. Student performance on standardized tests, ranging from state achievement tests to the Third International Math and Science Study[5], suggests that the goals of Science for All Americans—Project 2061[6], the *National Science Education Standards, NSES*[2], and the *Principles and Standards for Teaching Mathematics*[7] are not being realized.

Perhaps insight into this discrepancy between educational goals and student learning outcomes can be explained by surveying teachers' beliefs and practices. Because a single survey could not possibly identify all the aspects involved in productive teacher behavior, a narrower focus becomes critical. As such, the behaviors, beliefs, and motivations of mathematics and science teachers to implement inquiry-based learning situations are central to this study.

Inquiry-based instruction was the focus for this study because promoting positive conceptual change requires that student prior knowledge and preconceptions be engaged early and throughout the learning process[1, 8-10]. Such active engagement, promoted by constructivist learning theorists such as Vygotsky, requires that students go beyond learning facts, rules, algorithms, and procedures in order to become critical thinkers and problem-solvers. The researchers for this study chose to survey factors related to one specific instructional strategy, inquiry instruction, in an effort to answer the following research questions: How much time do teachers spend on inquiry instruction; how much do they believe they should spend on inquiry; and how are their behaviors, beliefs, and motivation regarding inquiry instruction related?

In the pages that follow, we provide a rationale for investigating inquiry instruction, we elaborate on the factors related to inquiry instruction that we investigated, and we discuss results obtained from the survey that we administered to all of the math and science teachers in GCSD.

Inquiry Instruction

Why should we focus our attention on inquiry instruction? Inquiry instructional practices have been lauded as central tenets for mathematics and science learning for over two decades by the *NSES*[2]. Further, numerous research studies and commissions report that K-12 science, technology, engineering, and mathematics (STEM) education can be improved through the use of inquiry instruction[1, 7-9, 11-13]. Nonetheless, teachers may or may not implement inquiry instruction in actual learning environments. This avoidance may be due to any number of factors. One reason is the complexity of inquiry instruction; in order to engage students fully in the inquiry process, teachers must help students to navigate several tasks, from brainstorming initial ideas, to gathering and applying information, to ultimately explaining results[14]. Similarly, teachers' reluctance to engage in inquiry instruction might be related to a lack of knowledge of or experience with non-traditional teaching methods[15], which could pose a barrier between teachers' desire to provide sound instruction and their motivation to implement a sound, yet unfamiliar strategy. Thus, the present study sought to investigate the reported behaviors, beliefs, and motivation for inquiry instruction of teachers.

For this survey and our subsequent work, we adopted a definition of inquiry-based instruction that unites insights from multiple educational theories and philosophers[2,8,16,17].

> *Inquiry-based instruction refers to the development of understanding through investigation, i.e., asking questions, determining appropriate methods, gathering data, thinking critically about relationships between evidence and explanations, and formulating and communicating logical arguments—adapted from the National Science Education Standards, 1996, p. 105.*

Two dependent variables were of primary interest to us in this study: 1) the percentage of time mathematics and science teachers report actually engaging students in inquiry learning experiences, and 2) the percentage of time they believe that inquiry should be used in the classroom.

Potential Factors Related to Inquiry Instruction

Several factors may be related to the typical amount of time teachers spend on inquiry in the classroom and the ideal amount of time they believe should be spent on inquiry in the classroom. Prior to the survey, we identified several of these, four of which are discussed below.

Grade Level Taught. A teacher's instructional grade level might influence the amount of inquiry-based teaching that occurs. For example, Keys and Kang[18] found that secondary teachers who have an interest in inquiry-based teaching possess both a personal and cultural belief structure regarding inquiry forms of learning. Conversely, Tobin and McRobbie[19] suggest cultural beliefs that permeate the secondary education setting, such as transmission, efficiency, rigor, and exam preparation, might be related to high-school teachers' avoidance of inquiry-based forms of teaching. More research is needed before generalizations can be made about trends in inquiry instruction across grade levels.

Support for Inquiry Instruction. The reasons vary considerably, but a teacher's perceived sense of institutional support for inquiry instruction might also affect its implementation. Spillane and Thompson[20] believe that a shift in instructional expectations stemming from true administrative support (or even mandate) might facilitate change, but a shift in policy alone would be insufficient for meaningful reform. Other scholars view teachers as more important catalysts in the change process than administrators or policy. For example, Hawley and Rosenholtz assume a *Lone Ranger* viewpoint[21], suggesting that teachers have a greater impact on student achievement than programs do. Similarly, even when programs are well-developed and have student success centrally-configured, teachers' active engagement within the program is critical to student achievement[22]. Thus, in this study, we investigate teachers' perceptions of administrative, peer, and curricular support for inquiry.

Self-efficacy for Inquiry Instruction. Self-efficacy refers to one's confidence in performing a specific task correctly[23]. Research on the motivational construct of self-efficacy has demonstrated the link between a person's confidence and subsequent behavior[24]. For example, teachers who are more efficacious are more likely to try new strategies and adjust current strategies, and they are more resilient when confronted with classroom challenges[25-27]. Consequently, teachers who have a higher sense of self-efficacy for inquiry instruction might be more motivated to engage and persist in inquiry instruction. Fortunately, self-efficacy is malleable, and improving teacher efficacy can be achieved with various experiences related to teacher development[24]. Because such a change in beliefs is critical to changes in practice[28], surveying teachers' self-efficacy for inquiry instruction might provide evidence of varying teacher motivation. This measurement might provide justification for conducting interventions designed to boost teachers' self-efficacy, and ultimately increase their motivation for inquiry and willingness to change their instructional practices.

Subject Matter Content Knowledge Training. The amount of subject matter knowledge (SMK) needed for teachers to lead inquiry learning has been a topic of debate for quite some time. Some researchers[29,30] suggest that professional development experiences focusing on SMK have larger positive effects on learning than experiences focusing on teaching behaviors. Lee[31] suggests that the quality of classroom interactions increases with teacher SMK, whereas teachers' reliance on textbooks decreases. However, Garet, Porter, Disimone, Birman, and Yoon[32] argue for a more balanced approach to teacher preparation, calling for inclusion of pedagogical training, while Lloyd et al.[33] suggest that SMK and pedagogical content knowledge (PCK) are not directly related. A practical resolution to this conflict is perhaps best summed up by Shulman: "Mere content knowledge is likely to be as useless pedagogically as content-free skill"[34]. Thus, there are conflicting views as to whether SMK is sufficient to promote quality inquiry-based teaching. Perhaps, PCK is more critical, as PCK entails the knowledge that makes the discipline comprehensible and understandable to others. But PCK can be seen as the confluence of SMK, pedagogical knowledge, and knowledge of context (student, school, and community)[35]. Again, more investigation addressing the relationships among these forms of knowledge and teacher behavior is needed.

The purpose of this survey study was to examine the relationships among teachers' inquiry behaviors, beliefs, and motivation and the factors previously described. Behaviors related to inquiry instruction were gathered through a self-report of the typical percentage of class time devoted to inquiry. Beliefs regarding inquiry instruction were gathered through various self-report and Likert-type items. Motivation was measured through a researcher-developed self-efficacy scale. Demographic information gathered included the teachers' highest degree earned, grade levels taught, years experience in the field of teaching, and so on. The next section of this paper reports the method of study.

METHOD

Participants

An entire population of K-12 mathematics and science teachers from one of the nation's largest school districts was surveyed for this study. The 1222 completed responses represented approximately 64% of the total district population of educators who teach mathematics, science, or both. Of the total responses, 173 were secondary teachers, 199 were middle school teachers, and 850 were elementary teachers. Collectively, 236 taught science, 283 taught mathematics, and 703 taught both. Participants averaged 12.8 years of teaching experience with 56% possessing a master's degree or higher.

Instrument

The survey instrument included 16 demographic questions; 17 Likert-scaled items measuring beliefs about inquiry instruction, content standards, and support structures; and 10 items measuring how often teachers engaged in inquiry and the frequency with which they made career connections during instruction. Of the four potential predictor variables described above, two were composite measures. Self-efficacy was measured with a composite of four items, while three areas (administrative, faculty, and curricular) were targeted for the variable measuring perceived support for inquiry instruction. Two dependent variables were measured for this study: 1) the typical amount of instructional time devoted to inquiry instruction, and 2) the ideal amount of instructional time that should be spent on inquiry practices.

RESULTS

Collectively, the mean percentage of time that teachers reported devoting to inquiry (TypInq%) was 39%. The mean percentage of time that teachers reported that they should ideally devote to inquiry (IdealInq%) was 57%. These measures, along with a look at their connection to the previously identified potential factors related to inquiry instruction and other independent variables, are discussed in the paragraphs below.

Grade Level Taught

A significant difference was found between teachers' grade level taught and their self-reported percentage of time spent on inquiry instruction (see Figure 1-1). However, the strength of this relationship was small, accounting for only 3.3% of the variance. Likewise, a significant difference was found between teachers' grade level taught and their beliefs about the ideal percentage of instructional time that should be devoted to inquiry, though the grade level taught accounted for only 4.8% of the noted variance.

Figure 1-1: Percentage of Inquiry (Typical and Ideal) Used in the Classroom vs. Level Taught

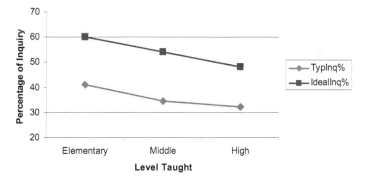

Content Area

Science teachers reported a significantly higher percentage of time devoted to inquiry during a typical lesson (37%) than mathematics teachers (34%). Further, science teachers reported a significantly higher ideal percentage of instructional time that should be devoted to inquiry (55%) than mathematics teachers (51%). Though these differences were expected, controlling for grade level revealed some surprises.

At the elementary level, the typical and ideal percentages of time allocated to inquiry instruction were significantly higher for science teachers than for math teachers. However, these differences disappeared for middle school teachers. For the high school teachers, both the typical and ideal percentages of time allocated to inquiry instruction were significantly higher for mathematics teachers than they were for science teachers. Also of note was that, as grade level increased from elementary to middle to high, both the typical and ideal percentages of time allocated to inquiry decreased dramatically for the science teachers, but remained approximately the same for the mathematics teachers. See Figure 1-2 and Table 1-1 for a summary of these results.

Figure 1-2: Percentage of Inquiry in Science and Mathematics Classrooms vs. Level Taught

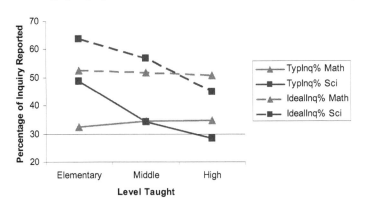

Table 1-1: Mean percentage of inquiry reported for teachers at various grade levels

	TypInq%		
	Math	Science	Comparison
Elementary	32.3%	48.8%	$t(134)=5.35$***
Middle	34.4%	34.3%	$t(197)=-0.035$ (NS)
High School	34.7%	28.5%	$t(171)=-2.40$*

	IdealInq%		
	Math	Science	Comparison
Elementary	52.6%	63.6%	$t(145)=3.45$***
Middle	51.7%	56.8%	$t(197)=1.90$ (NS)
High School	50.6%	44.8%	$t(171)=-2.00$*

NS indicates $p > 0.05$, *$p < 0.05$, ***$p < 0.001$.

effect support staff
most impt in elementary
Inquiry-Based Instruction   15

Support for Inquiry Instruction

Significant positive correlations were noted overall between the support scale (administrative and peer) and both the percentage of time devoted to inquiry during a typical lesson and ideal percentage of instructional time that should be devoted to inquiry reported by teachers. These correlations approached a medium level of significance[36]. When data were further analyzed by grade level, these correlations continued for all grade levels except high school. The highest correlation was noted among the elementary teachers, suggesting that support of colleagues and administration plays a more important role in the amount of inquiry that occurs in elementary classrooms than for middle and high school teachers.

Significance was also noted when studying the correlations between the role that curriculum support plays and the percentage of time devoted to inquiry during a typical lesson or ideal percentage of instructional time that should be devoted to inquiry. Positive correlations were found overall and at each grade level, and in all cases they nearly met or exceeded the medium level of significance. These findings suggest that the curriculum plays an important role in the amount of inquiry occurring in the classroom. Remember that this research addresses the role and frequency of inquiry in the classrooms of the teachers surveyed—not the quality or depth of the inquiry. No significant differences were observed between the correlations for math teachers and those for science teachers.

Self-Efficacy for Teaching Inquiry ✗ Effect

Correlational results suggest that teachers who possess a higher self-efficacy for teaching inquiry show a higher percentage of time devoted to inquiry during a typical lesson. This correlation drops only slightly but is still significant when controlling for level and content area taught. Similarly, those who report a higher self-efficacy for teaching inquiry show a higher ideal percentage of instructional time that should be devoted to inquiry. When grade level and content area taught are controlled for, the correlation drops slightly but is still significant.

Teacher Experience   No effect

Years of teaching experience. Even with the continued push in pre-service programs to encourage more inquiry and constructivist forms of teaching and learning[2], no significant correlation was seen between the number of years taught and the percentage of time devoted to inquiry during a typical lesson. However, without longitudinal data, we do not know whether professional development for in-service teachers has increased the use of inquiry to the same degree it has for pre-service teachers, or if there has not been a change at all.

Maximum Degree Earned. No significant difference was noted between the maximum degree held by the teacher and the percentage of time devoted to inquiry during a typical lesson or the ideal percentage of instructional time that should be devoted to inquiry.

Prior STEM Career. Those who had a STEM career prior to teaching reported a lower percentage of time devoted to inquiry during a typical lesson and believed that a lower ideal percentage of instructional time should be devoted to inquiry than those who had not had a prior STEM career. At this point, we can only speculate as to the reasons for this difference.

DISCUSSION

In terms of typical percentage of time allocated and ideal percentage of time that should be allocated, inquiry-based teaching and learning have assumed a prominent role in science and mathematics classrooms at all levels for the district surveyed. Yet current implementation of inquiry does not come close to matching the desired amount of inquiry. Teachers at all grade levels consistently reported believing that the ideal percentage of instructional time that students should be engaged in inquiry is about 20% higher than current practice (see Figure 1-1). This disjunct provides a great opportunity for future research.

Further, the typical and ideal percentages of time allocated for inquiry decreases significantly for science teachers as the grade level increases (see Figure 1-2). This trend is not true for mathematics teachers who show relatively static percentages of reported typical inquiry and ideal inquiry. Perhaps mathematics teachers perceive appropriate instructional practice in similar ways throughout K-12 education whereas science teachers do not. For this district, one conjecture entails that the state achievement tests in science place a heavy emphasis on the process or inquiry standards whereas mathematics achievement tests tend to measure more procedural competency. This may explain why higher inquiry is found in elementary science when compared to elementary mathematics. However, by middle school there is no significant difference between math and science teachers, but the state tests in science still emphasize both the content and the process standards. So, the argument used for elementary teachers no longer holds true for middle school teachers. At the high school level, significance is noted but now in the opposite direction—math teachers now report a higher percentage of time devoted to inquiry during a typical lesson and ideal percentage of instructional time that should be devoted to inquiry. The disordinal effect that was noticed between content area taught and grade level taught is a curious phenomenon where more research is needed. Perhaps high school science teachers lack the pedagogical knowledge to implement inquiry effectively at this level. However, why would high school science teachers have less pedagogical knowledge for inquiry than mathematics teachers do?

Though a definition of inquiry was provided on the survey *(inquiry refers to the development of understanding through investigation, i.e., asking questions, determining appropriate methods, gathering data, thinking critically about relationships between evidence and explanations, and formulating and communicating logical arguments—adapted from the National Science Education Standards, 1996, p. 105)*, it is possible that there remain large differences between mathematics and science teachers' understanding not only of what inquiry is, but what it looks like in the classroom. In other words, though the definition for mathematics and science teachers may be the same, science teachers may have a very different worldview than mathematics teachers in how inquiry is best implemented in the classroom.

Of the factors studied, self-efficacy for inquiry teaching, level taught, and institutional support were three areas identified that relate significantly to the percentage of time devoted to inquiry during a typical lesson and the ideal percentage of instructional time that should be devoted to inquiry. These differences are interesting because teachers' efficacy for teaching inquiry apparently does not differ significantly among grade levels or content area taught. These results suggest that self-efficacy is important but not individually sufficient to make the necessary transformation to more inquiry-based teaching[37, 38]. Further, the importance seen in the survey results regarding the need for strong support structures for teachers aligns with current research[22].

Possibly surprising to some[29-31] and not to others[32-35], prior educational and work experiences were not significantly correlated to the percentage of time devoted to inquiry during a typical lesson and ideal percentage of instructional time that should be devoted to inquiry. This lack of correlation brings into question whether professional development experiences are critical for effective teaching if devoid of specific pedagogical instruction[39]. Further research may be able to determine what a more effective balance between content knowledge and pedagogical knowledge is and if and how they can be better integrated.

Those with prior STEM careers before entering teaching typically bring considerable subject matter knowledge expertise because of their prior major and experience, but may have minimal pedagogical content knowledge training. Perhaps this is the reason that those with prior STEM careers actually report a lower percentage of time devoted to inquiry during a typical lesson and lower ideal percentage of instructional time that should be devoted to inquiry than their peers in mathematics and science education. Without the necessary content-specific pedagogical understandings, teachers cannot facilitate inquiry experiences that embed critical concepts within the learning experiences[40].

Training in subject matter knowledge and pedagogical content knowledge is probably not sufficient if self-efficacy and belief structure are not also directly addressed in the process. Changes in self-efficacy and beliefs may lead to changes in teacher practice, but teachers also need assistance and support in designing and teaching inquiry lessons so that lasting change occurs[28].

This study is based on results from a survey administered to K-12 math and science teachers. Although differences were significant among level taught and content area taught, dissimilarities are also likely to exist within disciplines for each content area. Through observations, professional development opportunities, and discussions, future research in this area can also prove valuable.

IMPLICATIONS

Based on our survey results, the grade level taught, the content area taught, the support structures available, and the level of self-efficacy to teach inquiry are all significant factors that relate to the percentage of time teachers typically devote to inquiry (TypInq%) and the percentage of time they believe they should ideally devote to inquiry (IdealInq%). Numerous implications result from these findings. Professional training programs that lack a long-term sustained commitment to change are not likely to affect teacher practice significantly and thus would have little impact upon student learning[41]. Even so, these programs are not likely to succeed unless they target specific grade levels and specific content objectives, ensure that appropriate support structures are in place, and directly address the teachers' confidence and beliefs about their potential for success. We hope that this study will help, at least partially, to guide the success of future professional development programs.

Other factors such as the highest degree held are not significant in determining the percentage of time devoted to inquiry during a typical lesson and the ideal percentage of instructional time that should be devoted to inquiry. This may suggest that graduate programs are not emphasizing inquiry instruction or are largely ineffective in doing so. Even if inquiry-based instruction is addressed in graduate programs, the efforts seem insufficient to promote significant change in practice or beliefs. Further, the reason for the difference noted in percentage of time devoted to inquiry during a typical lesson found between mathematics and science teachers is difficult to determine until one better understands what inquiry looks like in a science class as compared with a mathematics class. So, further research into the quality of inquiry being implemented in each of these settings is needed. But all else being equal, elementary science teachers report using inquiry to a greater extent and believe a greater percentage of time should be devoted to inquiry than elementary mathematics teachers do; middle grade mathematics and science teachers do not show a significant difference from one another for either variable; and high school mathematics teachers report significantly higher than science teachers on both variables.

This study and other research[22] show that administrative, teacher, and curricular support structures are highly valued for all levels of teachers and should thus be integral to teacher training programs. Even though the quality of inquiry being imparted in the classroom was not measured as part of this study, the data suggest that elementary teachers collectively use and value inquiry teaching at a greater level than middle or high school teachers. Pragmatically, this may show a perception among teachers that inquiry is either more important for lower grade levels or less feasible for higher-grade levels. We expected this to hold true for both mathematics and science teachers, though we had prior evidence of this only in science[19]; we found no studies in mathematics that addressed this issue. However, whether inquiry for the elementary grades is used to build deeper understanding of important scientific and mathematical concepts or simply to engage students in enjoyable activities without significant conceptual development is a matter for future study. Further, teachers in the upper grades may feel a greater need to impart learning in less inquiry-based formats, perhaps opting for what they view as greater efficiency, rigor, test preparation, and transmission. The reasons high school science teachers actually use and believe they should employ inquiry-based strategies less than elementary teachers is worthy of future exploration. Researchers in mathematics education are provided a very different problem—explain the relatively static view from all levels of mathematics teachers regarding the use and belief of how much inquiry-based teaching should be employed.

An argument often espoused by teachers for less inquiry teaching is that there is little time for it with all the content that must be "covered." If we are going to make significant strides in transforming how science and math are learned in school, particularly in the upper grades, then we first need to combat the dichotomization of content and inquiry where teachers feel that one is achieved only at the expense of the other. Perhaps one path to addressing this is to engage teachers in meaningful discussions as to what science and mathematics actually are and why students should study them. Certainly the standards in both disciplines suggest that the processes inherent in science and mathematics are critical, that students should master the scientific processes and learn to reason logically and critically. Subsequently, we might then direct efforts toward helping teachers to become more proficient at explicitly integrating key content (conceptual ideas) into inquiry learning situations. If teaching practice is to match teacher beliefs, the efforts must be sustained and provide the long-term support for teachers to practice and refine newly assimilated inquiry-based learning approaches[28, 42]. Further studies need to address the quality of the inquiry learning that is transpiring in the classroom as well as how content and inquiry can be better integrated from a practitioner's perspective.

With such a large percent of time that teachers already report spending on inquiry-based practices and with a desire to increase this amount significantly more, we found that the results, coupled with our other work with the district, brought into question the quality of the self-reported inquiry that was occurring. After we developed a tool to assess the quality, our observations and interactions verified that the quality was not generally at a level of proficient or better, so our work became focused on finding ways to better support teachers in improving as well as increasing the amount of inquiry they use in the classroom. Specifically, we established a common instructional framework (Chapter 2); created a Dynamic Web Tool to support planning, implementation, and reflection of inquiry practice (Chapter 3); and modified our protocol (EQUIP) so that teachers and other math and science leaders could assess and guide their own development of practice (Chapters 4 and 7).

In the chapters that follow, we hope that you will find information that will support your transition to inquiry-based practice, sustain changes you have already made, or help others as they move toward inquiry-based instruction. The evidence suggests that by doing so, your students will learn math and science at deeper levels and retain more of what they have learned. In short, they will be better positioned to tackle the exciting developments that the future has in store for all of us.

ENDNOTES

1.   Donovan, M. S.; Bransford, J. D., *How students learn: history, mathematics, and science in the classroom*. National Academies Press: Washington, DC, 2005.

2.   National Research Council, *National science education standards*. National Academies Press: Washington, DC, 1996.

3.   Wiggins, G.; McTighe, J., *Understanding by design*. ASCD: Alexandria, VA, 1998.

4.   Marshall, J. C.; Horton, B.; Igo, B. L.; Switzer, D. M., K-12 science and mathematics teachers' beliefs about and use of inquiry in the classroom *International Journal of Science and Mathematics Education* 2009, 7, (3), 575-596.

5.   Schmidt, W. H.; McNight, C. C.; Raizen, S. A. A splintered vision: An investigation of U.S. science and mathematics education. http://imc.lisd.k12.mi.us/MSC1/Timms.html

6.   American Association for the Advancement of Science, *Benchmarks for science literacy*. Oxford University Press: New York, 1993.

7.   National Council of Teachers of Mathematics, *Principles and standards for school mathematics*. NCTM, Inc.: Reston, VA, 2000.

8.   Bransford, J. D.; Brown, A. L.; Cocking, R. R., *How people learn: Brain, mind, experience, and school*. National Academies Press: Washington, DC, 1999.

9.   Bybee, R. W.; Taylor, J. A.; Gardner, A.; Scotter, P. V.; Powell, J. C.; Westbrook, A.; Landes, N. *The BSCS 5E instructional model: Origins, effectiveness, and applications*; BSCS: Colorado Springs, June-July, 2006; p 49.

10.   Willingham, D., Why students think they understand--When they don't. *American Educator* 2003, Winter 38-41, 48.

11.   Llewellyn, D., *Inquiry within: Implementing inquiry-based science standards*. Corwin Press: Thousand Oaks, CA, 2002.

12.   National Commission on Excellence in Education *A nation at risk: An imperative for educational reform*; US Department of Education: Washington, DC, 1983.

13.   National Commission on Mathematics and Science Teaching, *Before its too late: A report to the nation from the National Commission on Mathematics and Science Teaching for the 21st Century*. U.S. Department of Education: Washington, DC, 2000.

14.   Puntambekar, S.; Stylianou, A.; Goldstein, J., Comparing classroom enactments of an inquiry curriculum: Lessons learned from two teachers. *The Journal of the Learning Sciences* 2007, 16, (1), 81-130.

15.   Borko, H.; Putman, R. T., Learning to teach. In *Handbook of Research in Educational Psychology*, D. Berliner & R. Calfee, Ed. MacMillian: NY, 1996.

16.   Dewey, J., *Experience and education*. Collier Books: New York, 1938.

17.   National Council of Teachers of Mathematics *Technology conference: NCTM Standards 2000*; Arlington, VA, 1998.

18.   Keys, C. W.; Kang, N. H. In *Secondary science teachers' beliefs about inquiry: A starting place for reform*, National Association for Research in Science Teaching, New Orleans, 2000; New Orleans, 2000.

19.   Tobin, K.; McRobbie, C. J., Cultural myths as constraints to the enacted science curriculum. *Science Education* 1996, 80, (2), 223-241.

20.   Spillane, J. P.; Thompson, C. L., Reconstucting conceptions of local capacity: The local education agency's capacity for ambitious instructional reform. *Educational Evaluation and Policy Analysis* 1997, 19, (2), 185-203.

21.   Hawley, W. D.; Rosenholtz, S., Good schools: A synthesis of research on how schools influence student achievement. *Peabody Journal of Education* 1984, 4, 1-178.

22   Inquiry-Based Instruction

22.   DuFour, R.; DuFour, R.; Eaker, R.; Karhanek, G., *Whatever it takes: How professional learning communities respond when kids don't learn*. National Educational Service: Bloomington, IN, 2004.

23.   Bandura, A., *Self-efficacy and the exercise of control*. W.H. Freeman: New York, 1997.

24.   Woolfolk, A., *Educational Psychology*. 9th ed.; Allyn & Bacon: Boston, 2004.

25.   Hoy, W.; Woolfolk, A., Teachers' sense of efficacy and the organizational health of schools. *Elementary School Journal* 1993, 93, (4), 355-372.

26.   Tschannen-Moran, M.; Hoy, A., Teacher efficacy: Capturing an elusive construct. *Teaching and Teacher Education* 2001, 17, (7), 783-805.

27.   Woolfolk, A.; Hoy, W., Prospective teachers' sense of efficacy and beliefs about control. *Journal of Educational Psychology* 1990, 82, (1), 81-91.

28.   Jones, G. M.; Carter, G., Science teacher attitudes and beliefs. In *Handbook of research on science education*, Abell, S. K.; Lederman, N. G., Eds. Lawrence Erlbaum Associates: Mahwah, NJ, 2007.

29.   Corcoran, T. B. *Transforming professional development for teachers: A guide for state policymakers*; National Governors' Association: Washington, DC, 1995.

30.   Kennedy, M. M. In *The relevance of content in inservice teacher education*, American Educational Research Association, San Diego, 1998; San Diego, 1998.

31.   Lee, O., Subject matter knowledge, classroom management, and instructional practices in middle school science classrooms. *Journal of Research in Science Teaching* 1995, 32, 423-440.

32.   Garet, M. S.; Porter, A. C.; Desimone, L.; Birman, B. F.; Yoon, K. S., What makes professional development effective? Results from a National Sample of Teachers. *American Educational Research Journal* 2001, 38, (4), 915-945.

33.   Lloyd, J. K.; Smith, R. G.; Ray, C. L.; Khang, G. N.; Kam Wah, L. L.; Sai, C. L., Subject knowledge for science teaching at primary level: A comparison of pre-service teachers in England and Singapore. *International Journal of Science Education* 1998, 20, 521-532.

34.   Shulman, L. S., Those who understand: knowledge growth in teaching. *Educational Researcher* 1986, 15, (2), 4-14.

35.   Abell, S. K., Research on science teacher knowledge. In *Handbook of research on science education*, Abell, S. K.; Lederman, N. G., Eds. Lawrence Erlbaum Associates: Mahwah, NJ, 2007.

36.   Cohen, J., *Statistical power analysis for the behavioral sciences*. 2nd ed.; Lawrence Earlbaum Associates: Hilsdale, NJ, 1988.

37.   Ernest, P., The knowledge, beliefs and attitudes of the mathematics teacher: A model. *Journal of Education for Teaching* 1989, 15, (1), 13-33.

38.   Lerman, S. In *The psychology of mathematics teacher learning: In search of theory*, 21st Meeting of the International Group for the Psychology of Mathematics Education, Lahti, Finland, 1997; Pehkonnen, E., Ed. Lahti, Finland, 1997; pp 200-207.

39.   Shulman, L. S., Knowledge and teaching: Foundations of the new reform. *Harvard Educational Review* 1987, 57, (1), 1-22.

40.   Reynolds, A., The knowledge base for beginning teachers: Education professionals' expectations versus research findings on learning to teach. *Elementary School Journal* 1995, 95, (3), 199-221.

41.   Supovitz, J. A.; Turner, H., The effects of professional development on science teaching practices and classroom culture. *Journal of Research in Science Teaching* 2000, 37, (9), 963-980.

42.   Supovitz, J. A.; Mayer, D. P.; Kahle, J. B., Promoting inquiry-based instructional practice: The longitudinal impact of professional development in the context of systemic reform. *Educational Policy* 2000, 14, 331-356.

CHAPTER 2

THE 4E X 2: A MODEL FOR LEADING INQUIRY-BASED INSTRUCTION

If teachers are to adopt an inquiry-based practice, a framework is needed to support their efforts. This framework must be dynamic enough to adapt to the various instructional settings found in classrooms and schools throughout the nation. Though several models exist, we sought a research-based model that would improve the quality of instruction and increase student achievement. Our efforts resulted in the 4E x 2 (read "4E by 2") Instructional Model, which unites four major components of inquiry-based instruction (Engage, Explore, Explain, Extend) with formative assessment and reflective practice.

For clarity, we restate the definition that we have adopted for "inquiry":

Inquiry-based instruction is the development of understanding through investigation, i.e., asking questions, determining appropriate methods, gathering data, thinking critically about relationships between evidence and explanations, and formulating and communicating logical arguments—adapted from the National Science Education Standards, 1996, p. 105).

HISTORICAL OVERVIEW OF INQUIRY INSTRUCTIONAL MODELS

Since the early 1900s, instructional models have become foundational to teacher education programs and classroom practice[1]. Instructional models proposed by Herbert, Dewey, Heiss, et al.[2,3] began this movement toward using scientific inquiry as a way for students to learn in science, technology, engineering, and mathematics (STEM) disciplines. In the 1960s, Atkin and Karplus[4] introduced the learning cycle with three phases: Exploration, Invention, and Discovery. During the 1980s, Bybee[5] introduced the 5E Instructional Model that has gained in popularity across the science education community. The 5E Model includes Engagement, Exploration, Explanation, Elaboration, and Evaluation. Eisenkraft[6] added two more phases (Elicitation and Extension), resulting in the 7E Learning Cycle. Although these models have the potential to immerse students in inquiry-based learning experiences by creating a disequilibrium experience, a Piagetian notion[7], none of these models explicitly incorporates formative assessment and reflective practice, constructs that have proven to be effective and which, we believe, should occur during each stage of learning (inquiry). In the paragraphs that follow, we briefly explore these two additional constructs.

Formative Assessment

For us, formative assessment is defined as "encompassing all those activities undertaken by teachers ... which provide information to be used as feedback to modify the teaching and learning activities in which [students] are engaged"[8, p.8]. This definition is consistent with definitions used in other major works[9-12]. Rather than waiting until it is too late to help students who are struggling, teachers should use formative assessment to make informed decisions at each step in the instructional process, determining whether students are ready to move on or need some type of review or remediation.

Reflective Practice

Reflective practice refers to looking back and evaluating the degree of success of the instruction, classroom interactions, and learning that have occurred[13,14]. It also includes the self-awareness, understanding, and control of the thinking processes engaged in both by the teacher and by the students, aspects that are often referred to as metacognitive strategies[15,16]. Reflective practice is essential if teachers are to improve their instruction; quite simply, without reflective practice, teachers will not grow. The National Board for Professional Teaching Standards bases its certification largely upon the demonstrated abilities of teachers to reflect deeply and critically over their own practice[17-19]. For the purposes of the 4E x 2 Instructional Model, reflective practice specifically refers to teacher practice. Student reflection is also vital, but, in our model, it is subsumed within formative assessment.

THE 4E X 2 INSTRUCTIONAL MODEL

Figure 2-1 provides an overview of how the three major constructs (an inquiry instructional model, formative assessment, and reflective practice) interrelate. It will become evident later that not all four of the inquiry components have to occur in a given lesson, and they need not occur in a set order. However, in order for meaningful inquiry to transpire in the classroom, one aspect of the sequence is critical: students must have an opportunity to Explore before an Explanation of the major concepts or ideas occurs.

Figure 2-1. Interaction among the three constructs of the 4E x 2 Instructional Model [20]

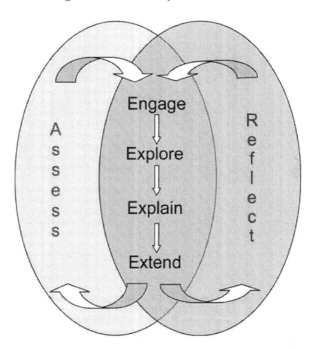

Figure 2-2 (on the next two pages) provides a template to guide planning when using the 4E x 2 Instructional Model[21]. Chapter 3 discusses and illustrates a Dynamic Web Tool that uses this template as the basis for planning. The different components of the Model are discussed following Figure 2-2.

Figure 2-2. Template of 4E x 2 Instructional Model

4E x 2 Instructional Model—Lesson Plan

Key Focus or Essential Question:
Standards Addressed:
Objective(s):
Materials:
Safety:
Sources/References/Ancillary Materials:

Reflect (R)	Phase of Inquiry	Assess (A)

Reflect (R)

Engage Reflection:

Check all that apply:
- [ ] What did student prior knowledge indicate about readiness to learn and existing schema?
- [ ] Misconceptions evidenced? How addressed?
- [ ] What interests or intrigues students? How can instruction incorporate these things?
- [ ] Role of students in forming scientific questions? How can questions be strengthened?

What is the post section decision? [ ] **Proceed;** [ ] **Quick Review;** [ ] **Remediate**
- [ ] Other:

Explore Reflection:

Check all that apply:
- [ ] Skillfulness of predictions made?
- [ ] Quality of study design and relation to goals?
- [ ] Conjectures being tested? Alignment of testing with the question/content being explored? How organized?
- [ ] Meaningfulness of data collected? How organized?
- [ ] Justification of approach used to solve question/problem? What justification tells about understanding?

What is the post section decision? [ ] **Proceed;** [ ] **Clarify;** [ ] **Remediate;** [ ] **Re-Engage**
- [ ] Other:

Phase of Inquiry

Engage

Check all that apply: [ ] Prior knowledge; [ ] Misconceptions; [ ] Motivation/Interest; [ ] Develop scientific question

Check Representative Questions:
- [ ] What do you know about...?
- [ ] What have you seen like this?
- [ ] What have we studied that might apply here?
- [ ] What have you heard about...that you aren't sure if it is true or not?
- [ ] What intrigues/interests you about...?
- [ ] What is confusing about...?
- [ ] What questions do you have about...?
- [ ] What would you like to investigate regarding...?
- [ ] Other:

Anticipated time needed to complete engage:
Description:

Explore

Check all that apply: [ ] Predict; [ ] Design; [ ] Test; [ ] Collect; [ ] Justify

Check Representative Questions:
- [ ] What if...?
- [ ] What would you expect to happen? Why?
- [ ] How can you best study this problem?
- [ ] What do you need to collect?
- [ ] How will you organize your information?
- [ ] How much data/information do you need to collect?
- [ ] What are some changes you noticed in...?
- [ ] Other:

Anticipated time needed to complete explore:
Description:

Assess (A)

Engage Assessment:

Check all that apply:
- [ ] Pre-test
- [ ] KWHL Chart (K&W)
- [ ] POE Model (Predict)
- [ ] Formative Probe
- [ ] Discrepant Event
- [ ] Warm-Up
- [ ] Brainstorming
- [ ] Science Notebooks
- [ ] Drawings
- [ ] Other:
- [ ] Other:

Explore Assessment:

Check all that apply:
- [ ] Observation
- [ ] Teacher Prompt
- [ ] KWHL Chart (H)
- [ ] POE Model (Observe)
- [ ] Record/Data Collection
- [ ] Graph
- [ ] Science Notebooks
- [ ] Other:
- [ ] Other:

Figure 2-2. Continued

Explain Reflection:

☐ Quality and accuracy of interpretation of results?
☐ Strength of evidence for claims?
☐ Effectiveness of communicating knowledge?
☐ Ability to see alternate explanations?
☐ Ability to verify procedure/results?
☐ Skillfulness in justifying approach/results?
☐ Ability to analyze the quality of exploration conducted?
What is the post section decision? ☐
Proceed; ☐ Re-Engage; ☐ Re-Explore;
Remediate; ☐ Have Students Clarify
☐ Other: ▨

Explain

Check all that apply: ☐ Interpret; ☐ Evidence; ☐ Communicate; ☐ Alt. explanations;
Verify; ☐ Justify; ☐ Analyze

Check Representative Questions:
☐ What took place?
☐ What changes did you notice?
☐ What visuals help to explain your findings? Explain them.
☐ What surprised/puzzled you? What is still confusing?
☐ How is this similar or different from...?
☐ What pattern(s) did you notice?
☐ How does this apply to what we learned before?
☐ Explain what happened?
☐ What has been learned?

☐ What evidence do you have for your statement?
☐ How would you explain...?
☐ What trend does the data show?
☐ How is your idea different from...?
☐ What do you mean when you say, "...:...?"
☐ Do you agree with...? Why/Why not.
☐ Where have you encountered a similar phenomenon?
☐ What do you think will happen if?
☐ Other: ▨

Anticipated time needed to complete explain: ▨
Description:

Explain Assessment:

Check all that apply:
☐ Whole Class Discussion
☐ Small Group Discussion
☐ Lab Report
☐ Oral Presentation
☐ Teacher Presentation
☐ KWHL Chart (L)
☐ POE Model (Explain)
☐ Other: ▨
☐ Other: ▨

Extend Reflection:

☐ Quality and number of applications made?
☐ Ability to elaborate on ideas/concepts?
☐ Skillfulness transferring knowledge to new ideas?
☐ Competence and accuracy generalizing experience?
What is the post section decision? ☐
Debrief; ☐ Re-Engage; ☐ Re-Explore; ☐ Another
Have Students Clarify; ☐ Another
Extension
☐ Other: ▨

Extend

Check all that apply: ☐ Apply; ☐ Elaborate; ☐ Transfer; ☐ Generalize

Check Representative Questions:
☐ What would happen if...?
☐ How do you think... applies to...?
☐ Explain from another viewpoint.
☐ How can this be used in the real world?

☐ What questions/problems are still unresolved?
☐ What decisions need to be made? What consequences/benefits/risks accompany certain decisions?
☐ Other: ▨

Anticipated time needed to complete extend: ▨
Description:

Extend Assessment:

Check all that apply:
☐ New Investigation
☐ Elaborate on current Investigation
☐ Real-World Application
☐ Science Notebooks
☐ Other: ▨
☐ Other: ▨

Engage

Engaging the learner through an effective *hook, mind capture, or perturbation* provides motivation to initiate the learning process, but engaging students in inquiry-based learning is more complex than just considering student motivation. In the 4E x 2 Instructional Model, the Engage phase of inquiry requires that consideration be given to the following: probing prior knowledge, identifying alternative conceptions, providing motivation and interest-inducing stimuli, and developing scientific questioning. (Note that scientific questioning is fundamental to both science and math classes.) These four foci for the Engage phase are guided by a significant body of research[22-25]. The *NSES* emphasizes the importance of developing scientific questioning skills in students, stating that "inquiry into authentic questions generated from student experiences is the central strategy for teaching science"[23]. Further, bringing students' alternative conceptions and prior knowledge to the foreground is critical to facilitate the perturbation or disequilibrium experience necessary to begin conceptual development. In order to facilitate the various aspects associated with engagement, teachers need to be explicitly cognizant of how, once identified, alternative conceptions and prior knowledge play a role in the inquiry learning process.

Effective questioning is critical during all phases of inquiry-based learning. Effective questions to guide teacher facilitation during the four foci of the Engage phase include the following: 1) What do you know about...? 2) What have you seen like this? 3) What have you heard about...that you aren't sure is true? 4) What would you like to investigate regarding...? Intentional, effective questioning is necessary, but not sufficient, to determine if students are ready to proceed to the Exploration phase, if they need a quick review, or if they need remediation before investigation is possible. Further, effective questioning encourages students to become invested in the learning experience.

Assessments that provide formative feedback are critical before decisions to move on can be adequately considered. Formative assessments for the Engage phase might include pre-tests, formative probes[26], and/or KWHL charting[27]. Formative probes provide content rich scenarios to see where student understanding begins. A KWHL chart is a graphic organizer to help facilitate learning by asking the following: 1) What do I "Know"? 2) What do I "Want" to know? 3) "How" do I find out? 4) What have I "Learned"? The more commonly known KWL chart leaves out the critical step where students help design how the learning and the investigation will take place. Designing a procedure is explicitly addressed under the "H" portion of the KWHL chart. Integrating formative assessment into the engagement section of the inquiry framework provides teachers with a robust model for involving students in the three primary learning outcomes for inquiry-based teaching: conceptual understanding, the ability to perform scientific inquiry, and an understanding about inquiry[28]. Assessment strategies for the Engage component include a discrepant event, formative probe, pre-test, test for misconception, and KWHL chart. Many of these strategies require the students to think metacognitively—thus making them aware of their own thinking. This way of thinking helps teachers become more intentional about their practice and encourages students to take more ownership of their own learning. This process, in time, will help raise the achievement of all students—even more so for low performing students[8,28].

When teachers reflect upon what has occurred during the Engage stage, they can gain valuable information that informs their decisions for the next steps of instructional practice. For instance, by reflecting on "What did student prior knowledge indicate about the student readiness to learn," a teacher is challenged to address specific needs of students before plowing through more material. It may become evident that a class or a group of students is in need of some remediation before proceeding. Another option for the teacher is to work on a deficit (e.g., interpreting a graph, understanding energy conversions) as the lesson proceeds but before the lesson is completed. Regardless of the path that is chosen, the teacher is now making decisions that are based on data, with the intention of doing whatever is in the best interest of improving student learning. This is in contrast to just covering material and then finding out at the end that 60% of the students failed to understand it. Reflective practice allows teaching to be specific and targeted to the needs of the learner.

Explore

Once the Engage stage has been successfully navigated, teachers can lead students into the Explore phase. Critical aspects of the Explore phase include having students delve into one or more of the following: predict, design, test, collect, and/or reason[23,29-31]. Examples of effective questions to help guide the facilitation of these aspects respectively include 1) What if...? 2) How can you best study this scientific question or problem? 3) What happens when...? 4) What data/information do you need to collect? 5) Why did you choose your method to study the question or problem?

As in the Engage phase, formative assessment and reflective practice are essential for keeping students directed along a meaningful learning path. The assessments can be contextualized into knowledge and/or process centered domains that focus on individual, small group, or class-sized groupings. Further, formative assessment and reflective practice become meaningfully intertwined when individual responses are united with small and large group discussions. A common example of this is the think-pair-share learning strategy[32].

Often teachers limit themselves to an observational, fairly passive role when assessing student progress during the Explore phase. Although it may be beneficial to let students *wade-in-*

the-muck at times, teachers may want to assume a more active role by providing guided prompts to encourage individuals or groups to think more deeply about the investigation at hand. This encourages students to slow down and think about their interactions with the content and their thought processes. Additionally, having students assess their own progress provides teachers with critical information to better guide intentional instructional practice[33] while presenting excellent opportunities for differentiated instruction[34].

Reflective practice during the Explore phase may begin by reviewing the individual student entries in science or math journals or by reflecting on students' proficiency in responding to their completion of the "H" portion of the KWHL chart (How do I effectively study this question/problem?). If, for instance, data collection surfaces as the predominant concern, then the teacher might initiate a brief collaborative discussion with small groups that focuses on how to gather data in meaningful ways. Such interactions with students emphasize assessment *for* learning instead of assessment *of* learning. Note that the students play a pivotal role as the teacher reflects upon her practice. For the Explore phase, the teacher should be concerned with reflecting on ideas such as, "How successful were students in setting up a scientific study? How meaningful was the data that were collected? How well are students able to justify and defend their approach?"

At this point, we hope it is becoming clear that formative assessment and reflective practice have considerable overlap. In fact, when formative assessment and reflective practice merge, instruction is more informed. More importantly, students are continually updated on their progress in relation to their goals[33,35,36].

The unification of inquiry instruction, formative assessment, and reflective practice during the Explore phase intentionally encourages deeper understanding. All three components are central throughout the instructional process, and students and teachers no longer have to wait until the end of the investigation before knowing whether students truly *get it*[8,15].

Explain

Although the Model should be seen as dynamic, the framework for the Model is predicated on having the Explain phase follow the Explore phase. This framework minimizes teacher-centered confirmatory learning, which is often superficial, and encourages student-centered learning. During the Explain phase students begin to make sense of how the prior knowledge and alternative conceptions from the Engage phase align with findings from the Explore phase. This sense-making occurs when students begin to communicate results and evidence[23]. However, if explanation precedes exploration, which is typical in non-inquiry instruction, students are thrust into passive learning situations that rarely challenge them to confront deficits in prior knowledge or existing alternative conceptions. So, when Explore precedes Explain, inquiry and content can be united in highly engaging ways that help students reshape prior alternative conceptions in ways that align with their new learning[37].

During Explore, the process skills are emphasized as students grapple with ideas. The content then becomes central during the Explain phase as the process skills are used to support higher order thinking skills such as interpreting, justifying, and analyzing. Further, in this Explore-before-Explain model, students from diverse backgrounds and abilities now have shared experiences as a basis for their claims and ideas. Other prior experiences that students bring to class make the learning richer, but learning is accessible to all students because the data collected and observations made were experienced by all. At the core of the Explain phase and inquiry learning in general, students are involved in a recursive cycle between evidence and explanations. Ideally, the process skills and content become embedded together in the investigation.

Central aspects of the Explain phase include: 1) interpreting data and findings, 2) providing evidence for claims, 3) communicating findings (written, oral, using technology), and 4) providing alternative explanations for findings. Examples of effective questions led by the teacher during the Explain phase include: 1) What pattern(s) did you notice? 2) What evidence do you have for your claims? 3) How can you best explain/show your findings? 4) What are some other explanations for your findings?

Some assessments for the Explain phase include lab reports, presentations, and discussions. These assessments can be formative or summative depending on the implementation. If students are allowed to resubmit work or if they are directed to revise their work based on peer editing, then assessment becomes formative and emphasizes the learning process over the learning product. Rubrics should be clear in their requirements but provide flexibility to allow for individual and unique expression of ideas. The goal is to understand concepts and scientific inquiry—not whether students can fill out a worksheet properly. If interpreting data and providing evidence are central to a particular investigation, then students need to justify their claims using the documented data and results.

Improved learning has been noted when both formative assessment and metacognition are used to guide students[38,39]. When metacognitive strategies are employed with students, time is created for sense making during which students can reconcile new knowledge with prior knowledge. This gives the teacher valuable evidence to improve instructional practice. Further, students become mindful of their own learning and employ strategies that assist their own progression of learning. Graphic organizers such as KWHL charts and POE (predict, observe, explain) cycles[40] that began during earlier phases of the investigation can now be completed (e.g,

What have you learned? Explain your results.). Additionally, concept maps can be used in a new way during the Explain phase. During Engage, concept maps provide insights into knowledge gaps; during Explain, students develop links among new concepts, prior knowledge, and learned skills.

Reflective practice during the Explain phase entails analysis of things such as "How strong are the claims being made by the student? How well are students able to convey knowledge of key concepts? How accurate are the claims?" During the Explain phase, students begin to unite their prior knowledge with the investigation that they conducted. Though teachers should have a basic expectation for minimum performance for all students, it is also appropriate to challenge students to exceed this expectation according to their interests and background. This provides an excellent opportunity for teachers to differentiate instruction.

Extend

If learning is not reinforced and then internalized after the Explain phase, when conceptual understanding begins to take hold, then students may quickly revert back to prior knowledge and understandings (and possibly misconceptions) they held before the investigation. Providing one or more opportunities for students to apply their knowledge in meaningful and authentic contexts helps students to begin solidifying their conceptual understanding, developing a more permanent mental representation. Alternative conceptions are tenacious and must be repeatedly addressed before lasting change occurs[41]. The disequilibrium experience caused in students during Engage and Explore now begins to gain resolution as understanding and knowledge articulated during the Explain phase now is applied in the Extend phase to new situations and to prior concepts studied. The number of extension activities or amount of time devoted to this phase should be determined by the difficulty of the concept(s) being studied, the importance of the concept in the curricular framework, and the degree of understanding that has been shown by all students.

During Extend, students are asked to apply, elaborate, transfer, and generalize knowledge to novel situations. Appropriate questions for the Extend phase include: 1) How do you think...applies to...? 2) What would happen if...? 3) Where can this be used in the real world? 4) What consequences/benefits/risks accompany certain decisions?

Assessment strategies may include having students perform a new investigation that remains focused on the conceptual ideas being studied. Using science or math notebooks, presentations, small group discussions, or class discussions, students can explore deeper implications of their findings. At this point in the inquiry process, assessments often are seen only as summative. However, by providing formative assessment even at this point, teachers can encourage students to think more deeply about their work. For instance, students could be asked to address an area of weakness seen during a presentation as a notebook entry, or they could be asked to respond to the teacher's comments in one or more of their notebook entries.

Reflective practice is designed to address explicitly whether the content has been mastered or still needs work. This, of course, can provide valuable information to teachers as they make important decisions about what to do next and how to improve future instruction. During the Extend phase, students should have an opportunity to deepen their cognition and solidify their knowledge on a given concept. In this portion of inquiry, teachers are seeking to understand to what degree students are successful in transferring knowledge to new ideas and the quality of understanding that students can demonstrate. Reflective practice in this stage of instruction really is focusing on the degree of conceptual understanding. The importance of the concept to the subject should help the teacher determine the level of proficiency and the depth of understanding that is expected from all students.

DYNAMIC VARIATIONS OF MODEL

On the surface, it seems logical to proceed sequentially through the phases supported by the Model, have students demonstrate their knowledge and understanding, and then move along to the next concept. Though this may be the desired path, conceptual understanding does not always follow such a linear, straightforward path. Just as there is not one Scientific Method[42], the 4E x 2 Instructional Model supports a dynamic structure. While variations from the progression through Engage, Explore, Explain, and Extend for an investigation may be appropriate, these decisions should be purposeful, with the guiding principle being to follow the path that best supports strong the conceptual development being achieved by students. As we stated earlier, our one consistent admonition is that Explore should precede Explain. Several variations of the Model are possible— each with a clear rationale for usage.

Model 1

Engage-Explore-Explain-n(Extend) is the default or typical path expressed by the 4E x 2 Instructional Model. The "n" denotes that multiple Extend opportunities should be encouraged to support transference of knowledge to new ideas by incorporating prior knowledge. The decision for how many different extension iterations are needed could be based on the following factors: 1) depth of student knowledge conveyed in prior extend investigation, 2) where in the unit or theme the investigation occurs, 3) relative importance of concepts, standards, and skills to the overall goals for the course, and 4) if prior content, skills, and ideas that have been studied can be embedded into the essential focus of the investigation. So if students understand at a significant level and can apply the knowledge to several different situations, then the investigation should justifiably be concluded. If a new concept has been introduced that will be reinforced later by another related investigation, then minimizing the number of extension opportunities may be warranted. However, if students are not likely to see this information again, then employing several Extend opportunities makes sense. Likewise, if multiple concepts throughout the course overlap with the current concept being investigated, then multiple extend opportunities are encouraged.

Other Models

Additional variations of the 4E x 2 Instructional Model are possible, but variations need to be intentional and should be predicated on Explore before Explain. For instance, the teacher might lead three consecutive cycles of Engage-Explore-Explain before implementing a final Extend. This approach might be used when three closely related ideas are studied. For instance, displacement, velocity, and acceleration could be studied in three different investigations before students transfer their prior and current learning (Extend) to motion in general. Note that these could occur in either a science or a math setting.

Another variation might include Engage-Explore-Explore-Explore-Explain-Extend. This would be applicable when one scientific question is being explored several ways before students seek to explain their findings. For instance, students could investigate three different plant types before seeking to apply what they studied to a larger ecosystem application. In a math setting, students might study the patterns they find by exploring three different linear contexts before they embark upon explaining their findings. Note that Engage was used only during the initial iteration because alternative conceptions should be clearly known and continually addressed during subsequent investigations.

CONCLUSIONS & IMPLICATIONS

The three learning constructs (inquiry instructional models, formative assessment, and reflective practice) that form the 4E x 2 Instructional Model all have a positive impact upon teaching and learning[2,8,33]. Unifying the constructs into one coherent model provides teachers with a mechanism to focus their instructional practice on these core fundamentals that will improve their practice. While the 4E x 2 Model should be seen as a dynamic inquiry-based instructional model, it also provides an explicit reminder of the importance and interrelationship among these three essential components learning constructs.

Although we do not claim that the Model addresses everything regarding effective practice, we do believe that it provides a meaningful and coherent structure that helps teachers plan, implement, and assess their instruction. The Model implies that teachers spend significant time on lesson preparation and on implementing the lessons themselves, but we are confident that the result of deeper, more meaningful learning will pay dividends in the long run.

To support teachers in the use of the Model, we have developed a web-based system that guides teachers as they develop, implement, and improve their plans—see Chapter 3. We have also created a protocol for teachers and evaluators to assess and improve the quality of inquiry-based instruction that is occurring in the classroom—see Chapter 4.

ENDNOTES

1.   DeBoer, G. E., *A history of ideas in science education*. Teachers College Press: New York, 1991.

2.   Bybee, R. W.; Taylor, J. A.; Gardner, A.; Scotter, P. V.; Powell, J. C.; Westbrook, A.; Landes, N. *The BSCS 5E Instructional Model: Origins, effectiveness, and applications*; BSCS: Colorado Springs, July, 2006.

3.   Dewey, J., *How we think*. D.C. Heath: Lexington, Mass, 1910.

4.   Atkin, J.; Karplus, R., Discovery of invention? *Science Teacher* 1962, 29, (5), 45.

5.   Bybee, R. W. *BSCS 5E instructional model*; BSCS: 2002.

6.   Eisenkraft, A., Expanding the 5E model: A proposed 7E model emphasizes "transfer of learning" and the importance of eliciting prior understanding. *The Science Teacher* 2003, 70, (6), 56-59.

7.   Piaget, J., Piaget's theory. In *Carmichael's manual of child psychology*, Mussen, P. H., Ed. Wiley: New York, 1970; pp 703-32.

8.   Black, P.; Wiliam, D., Assessment and classroom learning. *Assessment in Education* 1998, 5, (1), 7-74.

9.   Bell, B.; Cowie, B., The characteristics of formative assessment in science education. *Science Education* 2001, 85, 536-553.

10.   Crooks, T. J., The impact of classroom evaluation practices on students. *Review of Educational Research* 1988, 58, (4), 438-481.

11.   Kluger, A. N.; DeNisi, A., The effects of feedback interventions on performances: A historical review, a meta-analysis, and a preliminary feedback intervention theory. *Psychological Bulletin* 1996, 119, (2), 254-284.

12.   Natriello, G., The impact of evaluation processes on students. *Educational Psychologist* 1987, 22, (2), 155-175.

13.   Wilson, J.; Clarke, D., Towards the modelling of mathematical metacognition. *Mathematics Education Research Journal* 2004, 16, (2), 25-48.

14.   Shepardson, D. P.; Britsch, S. J., The role of children's journals in elementary school science activities. *Journal of Research in Science Teaching* 2001, 38, (1), 43-69.

15.   Wiggins, G.; McTighe, J., *Understanding by design*. ASCD: Alexandria, VA, 1998.

16.   Sternberg, R. J., Metacognition, abilities, and developing expertise: What makes an expert student? *Instructional Science* 1998, 26, 127-140.

17.   National Board for Professional Teaching Standards, *What teachers should know and be able to do*. Author: Washington, DC, 1994.

18.   National Board for Professional Teaching Standards *A distinction that matters: Why national teacher certification makes a difference*; Center for Educational Research and Evaluation: Greensboro, NC, 2000.

19.   National Board for Professional Teaching Standards Making A Difference in Quality Teaching and Student Achievement. http://www.nbpts.org/resources/research (October 23),

20.   Marshall, J. C. 4E x 2 Instructional Model *Periodical* [Online], 2009. www.clemson.edu/iim (accessed May 15, 2009).

21.   Marshall, J. C.; Horton, B.; Edmondson, E. 4E x 2 Instructional Model *Periodical* [Online], 2007. www.clemson.edu/iim (accessed May 15, 2009).

22.   Bransford, J. D.; Brown, A. L.; Cocking, R. R., *How people learn: Brain, mind, experience, and school*. National Academies Press: Washington, DC, 1999.

23.   National Research Council, *National science education standards*. National Academies Press: Washington, DC, 1996.

24.   Driver, R.; Squires, A.; Rushworth, P.; Wood-Robinson, V., *Making sense of secondary science: Research into children's ideas*. Taylor & Francis Ltd.: London, 1994.

25.   Hake, R., Interactive-engagement versus traditional methods: A six-thousand-student survey of mechanics test data for introductory physics courses. *American Journal of Physics* 1998, 66, (1), 64-74.

26.   Keeley, P.; Eberle, F.; Farrin, L., *Uncovering student ideas in science: 25 formative assessment probes*. NSTA Press: Arlington, VA, 2005.

27.   van Zee, E. H.; Iwasyk, M.; Kurose, A.; Simpson, D.; Wild, J., Student and teacher questioning during conversations about science. *Journal of Research in Science Teaching* 2001, 38, (2), 159-190.

28.   National Research Council, *Inquiry and the national science education standards: A guide for teaching and learning*. National Academies Press: Washington, DC, 2000.

29.   American Association for the Advancement of Science, *Blueprints for reform*. Oxford University Press: New York, 1998.

30.   Llewellyn, D., *Inquiry within: Implementing inquiry-based science standards*. Corwin Press: Thousand Oaks, CA, 2002.

31.   National Council of Teachers of Mathematics *Technology conference: NCTM Standards 2000*; Arlington, VA, 1998.

32.   Lyman, F. T., The responsive classroom discussion: The inclusion of all students. In *Mainstreaming Digest*, A. S. Anderson, Ed. University of Maryland Press: College Park, 1981; pp 109-113.

33.   Tobias, S.; Everson, H., Assessing metacognitive knowledge monitoring. In *Issues in the measurement of metacognition*, Schraw, G., Ed. Buros Institite--The University of Nebraska: Lincoln, NE, 2000.

34.   Tomlinson, C. A., *Fulfilling the promise of the differentiated classroom: strategies and tools for responsive teaching*. ASCD: Alexandria, VA, 2003.

35.   Stiggins, R., From formative assessment to assessment FOR learning: A path to success in standards-based schools. *Phi Delta Kappan* 2005, 87, (4), 324-328.

36.   Marzano, R. J., *Classroom assessment and grading that work*. ASCD: Alexandria, VA, 2006.

37.   Carin, A. A.; Bass, J. E.; Contant, T. L., *Methods for teaching science as inquiry*. 9th ed.; Pearson: Upper Saddle River, NJ, 2005.

38.   Bransford, J. D.; Brown, A. L.; Cocking, R. R., *How people learn: Brain, mind, experience, and school (expanded edition)*. National Academies Press: Washington, DC, 2000.

39.   Costa, A.; Kallick, B., *Discovering and exploring habits of mind*. Association for Supervision and Curriculum Development: Alexandria, VA, 2000.

40.   White, R. T.; Gunstone, R. F., *Probing understanding*. Falmer Press: Great Britain, 1992.

41.   Hestenes, D.; Wells, M.; Swackhamer, G., Force concept inventory. *The Physics Teacher* 1992, 30, 141-158.

42.   Windschitl, M., Inquiry projects in science teacher education: What can investigative experiences reveal about teacher thinking and eventual classroom practice? *Science Education* 2003, 87, (1), 112-143.

.

CHAPTER 3

DYNAMIC WEB TOOL

Technology is both a blessing and a curse. The ubiquitous presence of technology now allows information, data, and resources to be summoned with a few effortless keystrokes. The search results can yield a pile of unfiltered curricular resources for teachers. However, to make the point, a recent Google search conducted of "energy lessons" returned 42.6 million hits. This blessing of quickly available resources now becomes a curse of not knowing what is important or what is of high quality. Which of these lessons are worthwhile? Which ones are appropriate specifically for your students? Which lessons lead to powerful learning and achievement?

What seems to be happening is that teachers are given the standards that should form the foundation for their instruction and then provided access to a multitude of resources, kits, guides, and curricular supports. Then, out of this potpourri, it is expected that great instruction and learning will somehow emerge. For example, in its attempt to support teachers, our State Department of Education has provided a series of webpages that identify many resources designed to help teachers "cover" each standard. What is missing from all of this is the intentionality of instruction. Specifically, instruction should not be based on another exciting handout, computer program, or activity. Rather, instruction should be based on the prior experiences, knowledge, and misconceptions of the learners; the goals and objectives; and where the students are in their developmental progression toward becoming independent learners. The bottom line is that we can and must do better than give students activities that keep them busy on a given topic or standard. When students become vested in their own thinking and learning, they begin to master the content at deeper levels, retain what they have studied, and transfer their knowledge to new situations.

Our attempt to make instruction more intentional and learning more engaging resides in a Dynamic Web Tool for teachers that is based on the 4E x 2 Instructional Model presented in Chapter 2. The dynamic nature of the tool allows teachers to create or modify standards-focused, inquiry-based lessons while meeting their unique needs and those of their districts. The large variety of options available to the user is discussed in the remainder of this chapter. The most recent version of this chapter can be found at our website, www.clemson.edu/iim.

Specifically, this chapter provides guidance for teachers and leaders on how to navigate the site, thus allowing them to:

- View lessons other educators have created
- Modify existing lessons to meet individual needs
- Create new inquiry-based lessons using the on-line template
- Share comments and lessons with other teachers
- Learn about additional options available to help guide better instruction
- Understand future plans for the site.

HOME PAGE

The Inquiry in Motion Dynamic Web Tool is found at www.clemson.edu/iim/lessonplans. From this initial screen (Figure 3-1), you can register, login, or view public lessons. Until you register, you are only able to view lessons that others have already created.

Registration is free, takes just a few moments, and provides full access to the site. To register, select the register tab at the top of the home page. Don't worry; you will not be placed on a mailing list! We created the registration process for several reasons: 1) to allow teachers to interact with one another, 2) to provide a specific space for each user's work, and 3) to encourage positive discourse since all posted comments include the writer's name and school. When you register, be sure to record the user ID and the password you enter. Forgetting your user ID will prevent you from accessing any work that you have done or saved. In the event that you forget your password, it can be reset to a new randomly generated password that is forwarded to you via email.

Once you have registered and are logged in, then the options expand to allow you to view all lessons (Public Lessons), modify existing lessons (My Workspace), or create new lessons.

Figure 3-1. Home Page for Inquiry in Motion Web Tool

Transforming K-12 science and mathematics education

| Home | Public Lessons | Register | About Us | May 11, 2009 |

Inquiry in Motion Lesson Plans

Log in

A dynamic lesson planning tool for K-12 inquiry-based science and math teaching and learning.

Username:

Password:

Login

Register Forget password?

Links to Standards

SC Mathematics Standards

National Mathematics Standards

SC Science Standards

National Science Standards

Latest Lesson Plans

Grade	Subject Area	Title	National Standards	
6-8	Science	Simple Machines in Ancient Egypt	Physical Science; Science and Technology	
6-8	Science	Metals and Nonmetals	Physical Science; Unifying Concepts and Processes	
3-5	Math	Place Value	Number and Operations	
3-5	Science	Just Passing Through	Physical Science; Science in Personal and Social Perspectives	
6-8	Science	Our Changing Earth	Earth and Space Science; Physical Science	

PUBLIC LESSONS

When the Public Lessons tab is selected from the Home Page (Figure 3-1), you find a large number of lesson plans that have been created by many different math and science teachers (Figure 3-2). The lessons are dynamic in the sense that they can be used as they appear or can be modified to meet your own needs. To narrow the list to only the most applicable lessons, you can search for lessons that have specified words in the title, or you can sort the lessons by grade band, National Standard, subject area (math or science), or some combination of the four.

Figure 3-2. Public Lessons

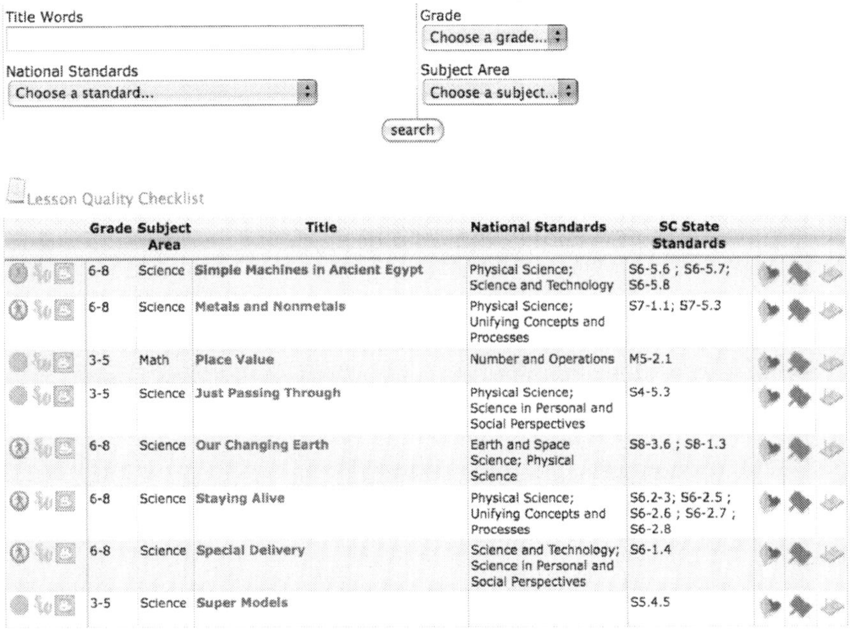

Title Words

National Standards
Choose a standard...

Grade
Choose a grade...

Subject Area
Choose a subject...

search

Lesson Quality Checklist

Grade	Subject Area	Title	National Standards	SC State Standards
6-8	Science	Simple Machines in Ancient Egypt	Physical Science; Science and Technology	S6-5.6 ; S6-5.7; S6-5.8
6-8	Science	Metals and Nonmetals	Physical Science; Unifying Concepts and Processes	S7-1.1; S7-5.3
3-5	Math	Place Value	Number and Operations	M5-2.1
3-5	Science	Just Passing Through	Physical Science; Science in Personal and Social Perspectives	S4-5.3
6-8	Science	Our Changing Earth	Earth and Space Science; Physical Science	S8-3.6 ; S8-1.3
6-8	Science	Staying Alive	Physical Science; Unifying Concepts and Processes	S6-2.3; S6-2.5 ; S6-2.6 ; S6-2.7 ; S6-2.8
6-8	Science	Special Delivery	Science and Technology; Science in Personal and Social Perspectives	S6-1.4
3-5	Science	Super Models		S5.4.5

Viewing a Lesson

Once you have selected a lesson from the Public Lessons, you arrive at a screen that provides all of the categories of the lesson in collapsed form (e.g., National Standards, Materials, Instructional Plan). To illustrate, we have selected a lesson entitled Simple Machines in Anient Egypt (Figure 3-3).

Figure 3-3. Collapsed or condensed view of a lesson

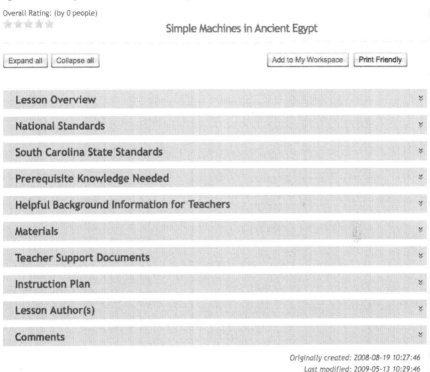

Expanded View of a Lesson

From this collapsed view, you have the option to "expand all" and view the entire lesson in full detail or to expand one or more of the individual categories by selecting the area(s) you wish to expand. In the next pages, we show the expanded view to illustrate the level of detail that is available.

Lesson Overview and Standards. The user proceeds through the lesson overview, which includes an essential question and key framing information. The standards are available at both the state and national level. We are currently making plans to alter the state standards section so that users from other states are able to add their standards just as easily as teachers in SC can currently add theirs. See Figure 3-4.

Figure 3-4. Expanded View of Lesson Overview and Standards for featured lesson

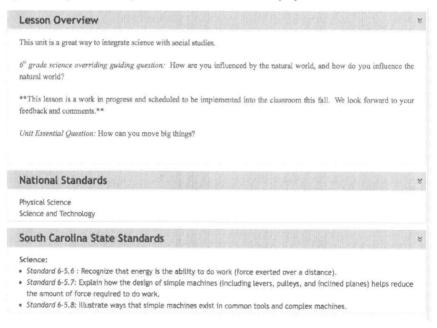

Materials. Each lesson provides a list of materials that are necessary in order to implement the lesson as described (Figure 3-5). The terms that are highlighted, which may be difficult to determine on this screen capture, have direct links to the listed items.

Figure 3-5. Expanded View of Materials for featured lesson

Materials

- Engage:
  - Science Journal
  - Ancient Egypt descriptive
  - Teacher costume (relating to ancient Egyptian royalty)
  - Paper
  - Pencils or colored pencils
  - White boards, markers and erasers (or other form to assess pretest)
  - Egyptian Music and picture
  - Pretest (Use as paper form, promethean board/PowerPoint form, etc.)

- Explore:
  - Box of "stuff" for each group formed (must include pulleys, levers, and inclined planes, other objects could include and are not limited to rope, batteries, other objects to assemble their pyramid, etc)
  - Pencils or colored pencils
  - Plain white paper
  - Rubric
  - Group Work Evaluation
- Explain:
  - Teacher created power point presentation on simple machines
  - Paper
  - Pencil
  - Key vocabulary handout
  - Children's literature – *How Do You Lift a Lion?* By Robert E. Wells

  Extend:
  - Internet access (laptop cart/library)
  - Digital camera for each group
  - Paper and pencils
  - Simple machine scavenger hunt
  - Possible Additional Journal Entries

Background and Supporting Information. The sections highlighted in Figure 3-6 provide areas that the lesson developers thought would be helpful to teachers: understanding of prerequisite knowledge that students need, helpful background information, and support documents to provide key resources for teachers. Teacher support documents provide teachers with tests, projects, assignments, PowerPoints, and URLs that are appropriate to be included in the lesson. Some of these resources include links to help teachers improve their own content knowledge before facilitating a given lesson.

Figure 3-6. Prerequisite, Background, and Supporting Information for teachers

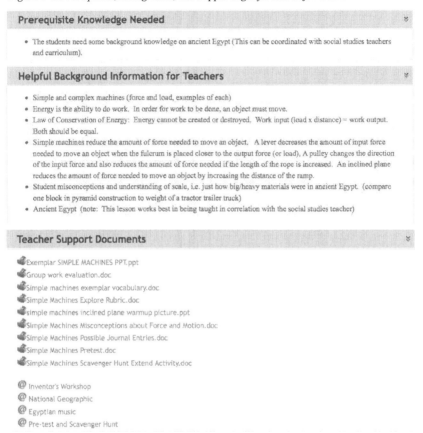

Prerequisite Knowledge Needed

- The students need some background knowledge on ancient Egypt (This can be coordinated with social studies teachers and curriculum).

Helpful Background Information for Teachers

- Simple and complex machines (force and load, examples of each)
- Energy is the ability to do work. In order for work to be done, an object must move.
- Law of Conservation of Energy: Energy cannot be created or destroyed. Work input (load x distance) = work output. Both should be equal.
- Simple machines reduce the amount of force needed to move an object. A lever decreases the amount of input force needed to move an object when the fulcrum is placed closer to the output force (or load). A pulley changes the direction of the input force and also reduces the amount of force needed if the length of the rope is increased. An inclined plane reduces the amount of force needed to move an object by increasing the distance of the ramp.
- Student misconceptions and understanding of scale, i.e. just how big/heavy materials were in ancient Egypt. (compare one block in pyramid construction to weight of a tractor trailer truck)
- Ancient Egypt (note: This lesson works best in being taught in correlation with the social studies teacher)

Teacher Support Documents

- Exemplar SIMPLE MACHINES PPT.ppt
- Group work evaluation.doc
- Simple machines exemplar vocabulary.doc
- Simple Machines Explore Rubric.doc
- simple machines inclined plane warmup picture.ppt
- Simple Machines Misconceptions about Force and Motion.doc
- Simple Machines Possible Journal Entries.doc
- Simple Machines Pretest.doc
- Simple Machines Scavenger Hunt Extend Activity.doc

- Inventor's Workshop
- National Geographic
- Egyptian music
- Pre-test and Scavenger Hunt

Instructional Plan. After the framing and support information, you will find a detailed instructional plan that follows the 4E x 2 Instructional Model discussed in Chapter 2 (Figures 3-7 thru 3-10). In this example, the instruction follows the following progression: Engage (Figure 3-7), Explore (Figure 3-8), Explain (Figure 3-9), and Extend (3-10). As discussed earlier, users have flexibility in determining the sequence and can have multiple components. However, as we emphasized in the previous chapter, there is one feature that distinguishes inquiry from non-inquiry lessons: students should explore in meaningful ways *before* they explain the underlying concept or have an explanation given to them.

True to the 4E x 2 Instructional Model, each lesson provides details about what and how the inquiry component is to be facilitated. For each phase of instruction, this includes representative questions, formative assessments that are pertainent for checking student understanding, and then reflective questions that are automatically generated to help teachers make intentional decisions about what needs to occur next in the instructional sequence and to improve their instruction.

Figure 3-7. Engage portion of Instructional Plan

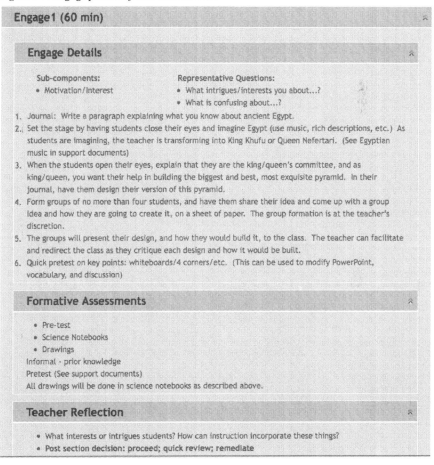

Figure 3-8. Explore portion of Instructional Plan

Explore1 (60 min)

Explore Details

Sub-components:	Representative Questions:
• Predict	• What if...?
• Design	• What would you expect to happen? Why?
• Test	• How can you best study this problem?
• Collect	• What do you need to collect?
• Justify	• How will you organize your information?
	• How much data/information do you need to collect?
	• What are some changes you noticed in...?

1. Give each group a box of "stuff," (be sure to include pulleys, levers, and inclined planes, rope, etc) and have them classify them into groups. Then have them explain why they classified the objects the way they did. (If time allows: Have students classify the items into different groups, and explain why.)
2. Have the students draw a design of a system to move a load, using the "stuff" from the box. (Remind the students that the load must move using this system, NOT their hands.) The design has to be approved by the teacher before the students begin construction of the system.
3. Students will build their systems according to their plan.
4. Journal: Reflect on what was done in class today. Prompt students by asking questions such as:
   a. Describe the process your group went through to design and test your
      system.
   b. What problems did your group encounter?
   c. What improvements could be made?
   d. Where is this process done in real life?
   e. What are some limitations of your design/system?

Formative Assessments

- Observation
- Teacher Prompt
- Science Notebooks
- Think, pair, share
Journal reflection
Rubric
Individual redesigned plan completed for homework.

Teacher Reflection

- Skillfulness of predictions made?
- Quality of study design and relation to goals?
- Conjectures being tested? Alignment of testing with the question/content being explored?
- Meaningfulness of data collected? How organized?
- Justification of approach used to solve question/problem? What justification tells about understanding?
- Post section decision: proceed; clarify; remediate; re-engage

Figure 3-9. Explain portion of Instructional Plan

Explain1 (60 min)

Explain Details

Sub-components:
- Interpret
- Evidence/Justify/Verify
- Communicate
- Alt.explanations
- Analyze

Representative Questions:
- What took place?
- What changes did you notice?
- Explain what happened?
- What pattern(s) did you notice?
- What surprised/puzzled you? What is still confusing?
- What visuals help to explain your findings? Explain them.
- What evidence do you have for your statement?
- How would you explain...?
- What trend does the data show?
- What do you mean when you say, ...?
- How is your idea different from...?
- What do you think will happen if?
- How is this similar or different from...?
- How does this apply to what we learned before?
- What has been learned?
- Do you agree with...? Why/Why not?
- Where have you encountered a similar phenomenon?

1. Regroup and present their final design that they did for homework, to the other members of their group.
2. Have a discussion explaining what was used to make moving the load easier; include real world examples of simple machines in use. Talk about work, and how simple machines make work easier. Include key vocabulary terms the students need to know and have the students come up with the definitions as a class. (Be sure to ask open-ended questions and allow for wait time. Address each answer with prompts for further thinking and guiding the discussion, such as: Why did you use...? How are you going to acquire...? How can you improve...? Etc.)
3. Use the teacher-made PowerPoint (see teacher support documents) to reinforce class discussion and key points, identify misconceptions, or give additional examples/scenarios.

Figure 3-9. Continued

Key Vocabulary: lever, pulley, inclined plane, force, work, load, fulcrum, complex machine, technological design, classify

PowerPoint:

1. This presentation is provided to use as a tool to justify, analyze or re-direct use with the three basic simple machines concepts for inclined plane, lever and pulley.
2. The time is flexible depending upon your students' needs.
3. Individual essential questions that could be used include: How can a slope help in moving a big object? How can you lift the teacher (insert your name)? How can a bunch of monkeys be lifted?
4. Each of the 3 sections of this presentation will include a small engage segment followed by the key concepts for each machine. All machines should focus around the Law of the Conservation of Energy.
5. Be sure to reference misconceptions (linked in resources section) throughout to keep these common misconceptions consistent and clear. If these can begin to be addressed now and understood, the remainder of the standard on energy forms, types and transfers should help with overall understanding.

Formative Assessments

- Whole Class Discussion
- Journals

1. Group discussion on key points.
2. Give back pretest and justify why they got the answer right or explain why they got the answer wrong. (They will have an explanation for EACH answer.)
3. Journal entry summing up what they have learned about simple machines, where they are found in real life, how they are used. It would also be helpful to include a diagram for each representing the key concept that "A simple machine should represent the Law of Conservation of Energy. Work input (load x distance) = work output. Both should be equal, as energy cannot be created or destroyed."

Teacher Reflection

- Quality and accuracy of interpretation of results?
- Strength of evidence for claims? Ability to verify procedure/results? Skillfulness in justifying approach/results?
- Effectiveness of communicating knowledge?
- Ability to see alternate explanations?
- Ability to analyze the quality of exploration conducted?
- Post section decision: proceed; re-engage; re-explore; remediate; have students clarify

Figure 3-10. Extend portion of Instructional Plan

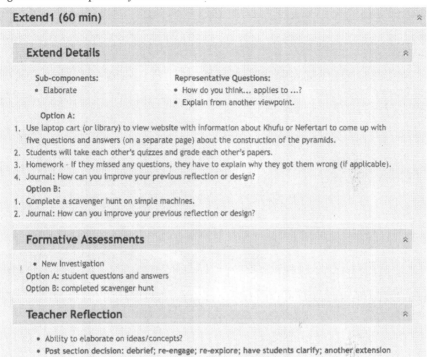

Extend1 (60 min)   ≳

Extend Details   ≳

Sub-components: Representative Questions:
• Elaborate   • How do you think... applies to ...?
                                 • Explain from another viewpoint.

Option A:
1. Use laptop cart (or library) to view website with information about Khufu or Nefertari to come up with five questions and answers (on a separate page) about the construction of the pyramids.
2. Students will take each other's quizzes and grade each other's papers.
3. Homework - If they missed any questions, they have to explain why they got them wrong (if applicable).
4. Journal: How can you improve your previous reflection or design?

Option B:
1. Complete a scavenger hunt on simple machines.
2. Journal: How can you improve your previous reflection or design?

Formative Assessments   ≳

• New Investigation
Option A: student questions and answers
Option B: completed scavenger hunt

Teacher Reflection   ≳

• Ability to elaborate on ideas/concepts?
• Post section decision: debrief; re-engage; re-explore; have students clarify; another extension

Comments. Below the instructional plan, you will find a section that lists the lesson's authors. Below this is a section that allows registered users to make comments and rate the lesson. Ratings are based on a 5-star system (Figure 3-11). Comments are for the purpose of justifying the rating and/or for providing constructive feedback regarding the lesson. For instance, a user may have liked the lesson and added comments to share how she adapted it to better address the needs of her students. Alternatively, she could have created a different version of the lesson as discussed later in this chapter.

Figure 3-11. Rating and Comments Section of Lesson

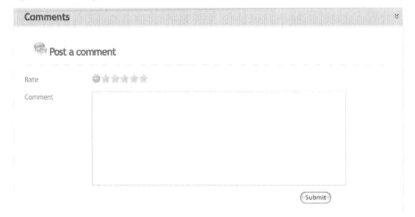

MY WORKSPACE

One of the things that distinguish this site from static sites is the My Workspace area where you can create or modify existing lessons—even lessons that were created by others. The MyWorkspace area (Figure 3-12) can be used as a:

1. Storage place for Public Lessons for later viewing or use.
2. Place where Public Lessons can be stored and modified to meet your unique needs.
3. Private location to store lessons that you have created but choose not to make public.

For new users, no lessons are found in the My Workspace area. Users can add lessons by selecting a lesson in the Public Lessons area and then selecting the option "Add to MyWorkspace" (Figure 3-2), which is the third icon from the right. Once a lesson is added to the MyWorkspace area the title becomes "Copy of [The Original Title]." This leaves the original lesson intact.

Figure 3-12. My Workspace

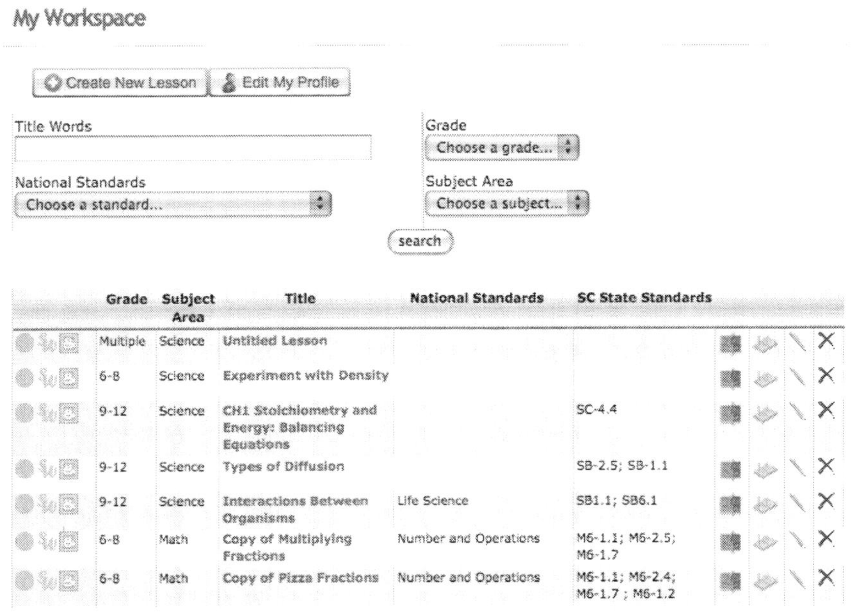

My Workspace

Grade	Subject Area	Title	National Standards	SC State Standards				
Multiple	Science	Untitled Lesson						
6-8	Science	Experiment with Density						
9-12	Science	CH1 Stoichiometry and Energy: Balancing Equations		SC-4.4				
9-12	Science	Types of Diffusion		SB-2.5; SB-1.1				
9-12	Science	Interactions Between Organisms	Life Science	SB1.1; SB6.1				
6-8	Math	Copy of Multiplying Fractions	Number and Operations	M6-1.1; M6-2.5; M6-1.7				
6-8	Math	Copy of Pizza Fractions	Number and Operations	M6-1.1; M6-2.4; M6-1.7 ; M6-1.2				

CREATE A LESSON

Once in the My Workspace area, you can select Create New Lesson (see tab at top left of Figure 3-12), which guides you through the lesson creation template. A saved lesson appears in the My Workspace area even if it has not been fully completed.

The final product of the lesson appears in the form shown in the example highlighting a Public Lesson (Figures 3-3 thru 3-11), but the template for creating the lesson is broken into discrete pieces that guide you step-by-step, which are shown in the next several figures. Figure 3-13 shows the author and title information. The author defaults to the user currently logged in. Additional authors can be added as needed. The user ID is needed for each author to be added, so if you're working with others, be sure you enter the correct ID. Additional authors may or may not be given editing rights for the lesson (though any registered user can always create a different version—a child—of an original). Any edits that are made to a lesson by an authorized author show up in the My Workspace of all authors. The next step is to add the Lesson Info, which includes a title, the discipline (math, science, or both), and the grade level (K-2, 3-5, 6-8, 9-12).

Figure 3-13. Creating a New Lesson—Part I

After entering the Lesson Info, you then complete the national and state standards that are appropriate for the lesson. We assume that the Inquiry (science) or the Process Standards (math) are among the National Standards included, so we use this area to identify only the relevant content standards. Next, you provide a Lesson Overview that contains a clarifying sentence or two, lesson objectives, and the guiding essential question for the lesson. The State Standards are currently limited to the South Carolina Standards but plans are being made to expand this to other states.

Figure 3-14. Creating a New Lesson—Part II

More Lesson Info

Title   Conservation of Mass

National Standards   Choose a standard...

                            Choose additional standard...

Lesson Overview

✂ 🗐 🗐 🗐 🗐 **B** *I* U | ᴬᴮᶜ ≣ ≣ ≣ ≣ ≣ ⋮≡ ⋮≡ ↻ ↺ ↻ ↺ ✓ ▾

SC State Standards

Please paste appropriate standard in the area provided:
South Carolina Science Standards
South Carolina Mathematics Standards

Standard Notation: [   ] Standard Type: ⦿ Science ○ Math

(Save standard)

The next step in creating a new lesson is describing Pre-Instructional Considerations (Figure 3-15), in which you describe the prior knowledge that students should have before beginning the lesson and any background information you believe would be helpful to the teacher. This might include, if appropriate, historical background, clarification of terms used in the lesson, common misconceptions, and any other information that would assist the teacher in becoming more comfortable and confident with the material. Then, a materials list is shared to help teachers know at a glance know what should be gathered for each team or class of students. Finally, you add all Teacher Support Documents, including documents that you upload and links to appropriate URLs.

Figure 3-15. Creating a New Lesson—Part III

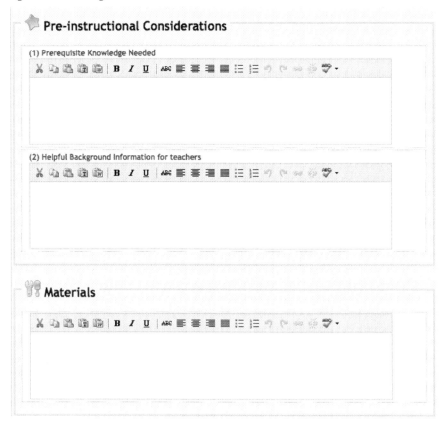

Figure 3-15. Continued

◆ Teacher Support Documents

Add a Document: *(Each file limit 10M, total files limit 100M)*

(Browse...) (Upload)

Add an Internet URL Link:

Link Title/Description: (Add Link)

Following all of the background documentation, you arrive at the Instructional Plan (Figure 3-16). (Of course, in some cases, you may prefer to create the Instructional Plan before adding all of the preliminary information and links; the system allows you to complete the sections in whatever order you desire.) Guided by the 4E x 2 Instructional Model (see Chapter 2), you select the appropriate component of inquiry and complete it. For instance, if New Engage is selected then the screen from Figure 3-17 appears. You are asked to complete six basic things for each component of inquiry: 1) an estimate of the time needed to complete this phase of inquiry, 2) the sub-components of inquiry that are addressed (these vary for each component), 3) representative questions for teachers to consider during instruction to improve discourse (you can check or uncheck these), 4) a succinct description for the component, 5) the formative assessments to be used to check for student understanding and to guide instruction, and 6) a brief description of these formative assessments.

The final lesson plan automatically includes reflective questions for the teacher to consider before progressing to the next stage of instruction. These questions are determined by the database and are based on the sub-components of inquiry that have been selected.

Continue to enter the various components until your Instructional Plan is complete. In the event that a component is misplaced or you choose to add a component later on, the order of the components can be reorganized (see Figure 3-16). Going to My Workspace, you can view the entire lesson that has been created in the final viewable form.

Figure 3-16. Creating a New Lesson—Part IV

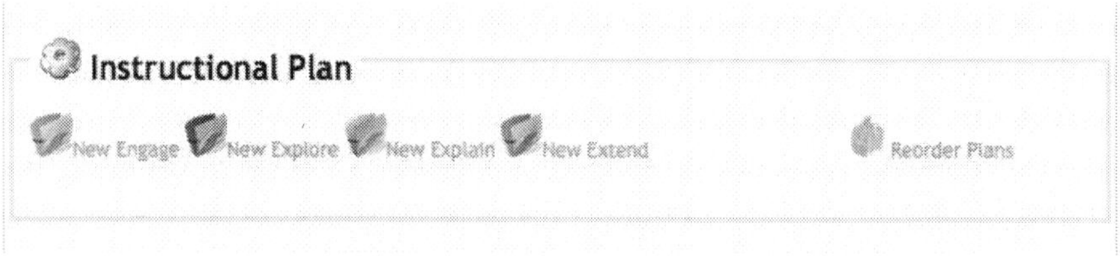

Figure 3-17 Creating a New Lesson—Engage Portion

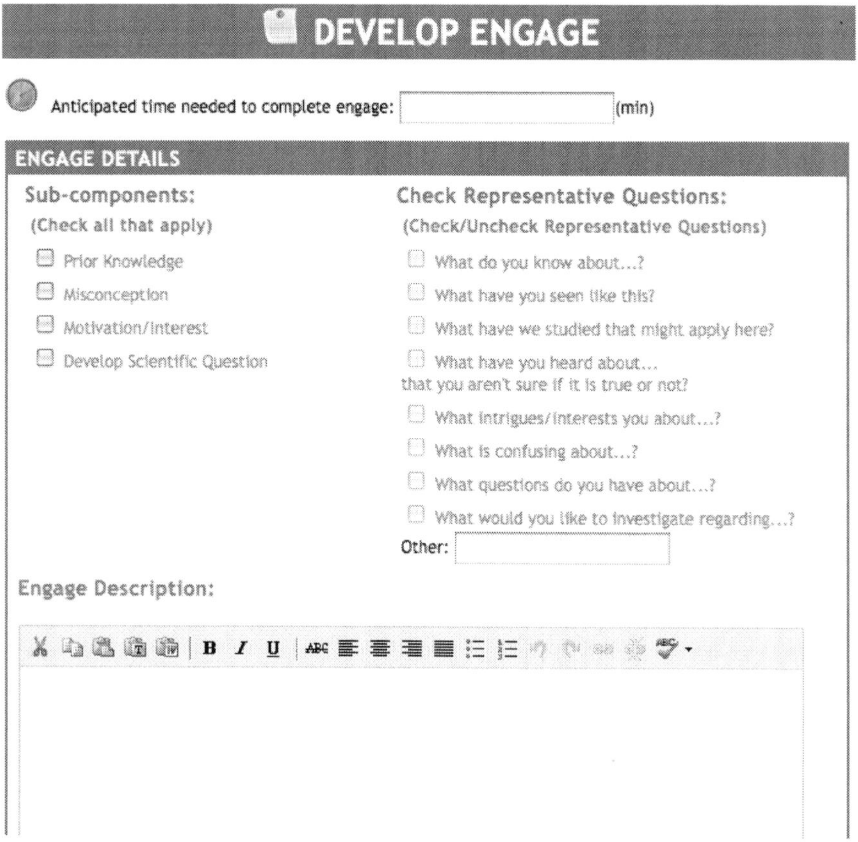

Figure 3-17. Continued

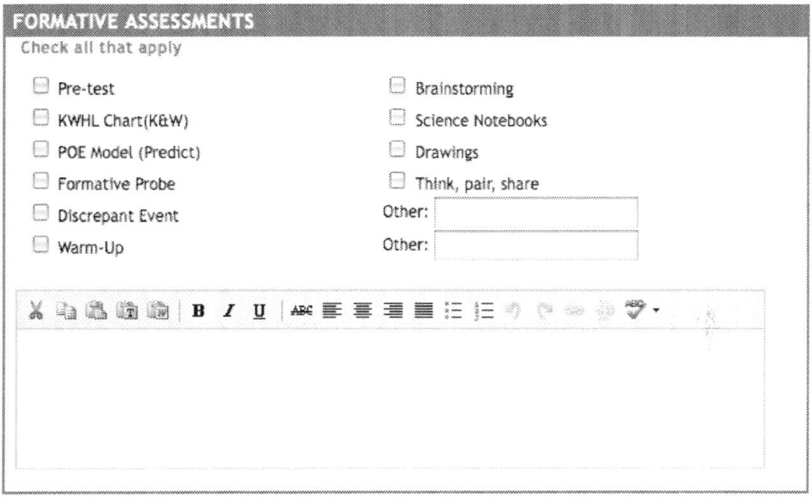

PUBLISHING LESSONS

Lessons in the My Workspace area can be published for all to see. If you are an original author and choose to publish the lesson to the Public Lessons area, then it will show up as a unique or "parent" lesson. If you choose to publish someone else's lesson that you have modified (see next section), then you will be prompted to identify what basic changes you have made. The revised lesson will show up as a "child" of the original—similar to a thread in a discussion board or blog. To publish a lesson, you must be in My Workspace and select the publish icon next to the lesson title (see Figure 3-12 fourth from last column). Lessons may be "unpublished," but to do so requires permission from one of the system administrators before it is removed.

MODIFYING OR EDITING A LESSON

Since lessons are not meant to be static, they can be modified and edited. Any lesson in the Public Lessons area can be copied to My Workspace and then modified. To modify a lesson in the My Workspace area, select the pencil icon (see second from last column in Figure 3-12). Whether or not you are one of the original authors, you can make changes to the lesson and then save them. If you are one of the original authors with editing rights, then any changes you make will be made to the original document when you Publish it. If you are editing a lesson created by someone else, then you cannot change the original, even when you publish it. Your changes will be to the copy or child of the original.

QUALITY CONTROL AND FUTURE PLANS

Our primary goal with this site is to provide a tool for teachers to find and create high-quality, dynamic, inquiry-based lesson plans that focus on key ideas in math and science. To this end, we have designed three components to encourage the development of lessons of high quality. As of this writing, only the first of these has been implemented.

The first component of quality control is a Lesson Quality Checklist (Figure 3-18) that we as system administrators use to screen all lessons that are published. See the first column of Figures 3-2 or 3-12 for examples. The options are no award, silver or gold. Lessons that have not been reviewed or have not earned a sufficient level of distinction receive no award. Lessons earning silver distinction are high-quality overall, but need some modification in one or two areas before they earn the top award. Gold is earned when all 20 of the criteria being measured have been successfully achieved (Figure 3-18). In addition, as mentioned earlier, teachers also have the opportunity to rate any of the lessons found in the Public Lesson area. Collectively, the Lesson Quality Checklist and the ratings for each lesson provide a broad perspective of lesson quality that includes input from curriculum specialists and professors in math and science education to practicing classroom teachers.

The second component that is designed to improve the quality of implementation is the student work samples section. A variety of work samples will be provided from various lessons to show teachers what different levels of achievement might look like. This feature will soon be added to the web site. When student work samples are present, an icon entitled SW (second column on Figure 3-2) will be illuminated. The work samples, which must be anonymous, will be found under the Teacher Support Documents. This will help both new and experienced teachers better understand what proficient practice looks like for the given assessments or assignments.

Finally, the third component designed to facilitate higher quality of implementation is a video or series of videos that show the lesson being led by a practicing teacher. When the video(s) is (are) present, the video icon will be highlighted (third column on Figure 3-2). The actual videos will be available under the Teacher Support Documents. This feature will also soon be added to the website.

Figure 3-18. Lesson Quality Checklist

For Exemplars to earn Gold Distinction, all criteria must be met. For exemplars to earn Silver Distinction, all essential criteria and at least 8 out of 10 of the important criteria must be met.

Lesson Title:

Criteria	Meets criteria	Doesn't meet criteria
Essential (all criteria must be met to receive gold or silver certification)		
National standards are clearly specified and aligned with state standards.	○	○
Sufficient background information is provided.	○	○
The instructional plan effectively addresses the national and state standards specified for this lesson.	○	○
Sufficient detail is given for each phase of the instructional plan to allow another teacher to duplicate this lesson.	○	○
Explore phases of the instructional plan precede explanations of content.	○	○
Lessons are largely student-focused with students taking an active role in learning.	○	○
Real world or meaningful context is embedded in the lesson to promote conceptual understanding.	○	○
Safety issues are addressed as necessary.	○	○
The lesson addresses a fundamental concept or big idea in either math or science.	○	○
Lesson is cohesive: standards, lesson, and assessments well-aligned.	○	○

Figure 3-18. Continued

Important (Gold=All 10 criteria met; Silver=at least 8 criteria met)		
A concise lesson overview is provided.	○	○
State standards are identified by number and description.	○	○
Prerequisite knowledge is addressed as necessary.	○	○
Necessary materials are listed.	○	○
All necessary teacher support documents are present and labeled appropriately.	○	○
The Instructional Plan includes engage, explore, explain, and extend.	○	○
At least one sub-component (e.g., prior knowledge) is specified for each phase of the instructional plan.	○	○
Formative assessments that will guide instruction are provided and described for each phase of the instructional plan.	○	○
Questions for teacher reflection are present for each phase of the instructional plan.	○	○
The lesson makes connections to other concepts in math or science.	○	○
Student Work		
Samples that display varying abilities are provided.	○	○
Video		
Video that demonstrates solid instructional practice is provided.	○	○

Over the last two years, teachers, researchers, computer specialists, and industrial engineering specialists have provided input for this site, which is designed to assist teachers as they plan, implement, and refine high-quality inquiry-based instruction. This collaborative framework is a work in progress that we will continue to modify based on the needs of the teachers who use it. Consequently, when you use the web tool, you may find it somewhat different from what is shown in this chapter. However, the fundamentals will not change, and we believe that this chapter will help you navigate the site. Our intention is to provide a highly supportive, free environment for teachers, schools, and districts to store and interact with exemplary inquiry-based lessons that focus on critical ideas in math and science. Our hope is that you will find this a valuable tool in your pursuit of improving your inquiry-based instruction.

CHAPTER 4

ASSESSING TEACHER PERFORMANCE
IN AN INQUIRY-BASED CLASSROOM

Excellence in instructional practice can be achieved when the teaching is intentional and guided by formative feedback. Intentionality is created when teachers reflect often on their instruction and base instructional decisions on student learning. One approach to teaching involves merely finding curriculum and activities to fill the class period all under the guise of teaching to a specific standard. This approach, though common, does not bring about significant learning for all—particularly for those who struggle in school. Instead, solid instruction begins by using the standards as a focusing mechanism for each lesson. Then, the curriculum, investigations, and interactions are based upon the needs and progression of the learner.

We can and must do more than just have students learn to parrot formulas, algorithms, and definitions back to us. Learning entails having students think critically about the material, make connections to prior learning, and apply ideas and insights to new situations. The key factor in achieving this is the teacher, and the evidence suggests that an inquiry-based approach can stimulate and develop critical thinking[1-4]. However, simply saying that one uses an inquiry-based approach is not sufficient to ensure that effective high-quality inquiry is being led.

So how do we assess the quality of the inquiry that teachers lead in their classrooms? How do we set out a specific plan of action for a teacher to grow and improve? This chapter focuses on a protocol we developed to assess teacher performance as it pertains to inquiry-based instruction. This protocol, which we have named the Electronic Quality of Inquiry Protocol (EQUIP), can be used as a snapshot to measure the quality of inquiry on several indicators for a given class or as a guide that outlines specific areas for teachers to target for growth. EQUIP provides a reliable and valid resource to measure the quality of inquiry that is being facilitated within classrooms. We researched, developed, and refined EQUIP over a period of three years[5]. Portions of this chapter are reprinted and adapted from an article entitled "EQUIPping Teachers: A Protocol to Guide and Improve Inquiry-Based Instruction" that originally appeared in *The Science Teacher*, May 2009[6].

INTRODUCTION

Many teachers have uttered the following, or at least something similar: "I don't know exactly how to define inquiry, but I know it when I see it." This intuitive understanding may work for onlookers, but something greater is needed from those who lead instruction in our classrooms. In previous chapters, we cited the definition of inquiry that has guided us:

> *Inquiry-based instruction is the development of understanding through investigation, i.e., asking questions, determining appropriate methods, gathering data, thinking critically about relationships between evidence and explanations, and formulating and communicating logical arguments—adapted from the National Science Education Standards, p.105[7].*

Even with this definition, however, the steps that mathematics and science teachers should take in designing, implementing, and assessing inquiry-based instruction are not necessarily clear. The 4E x 2 Instructional Model[8,9] (Chapter 2), with the support of the Dynamic Web Tool (Chapter 3), helps tremendously with lesson design and implementation. We look to EQUIP for assessing inquiry-based instruction. Only if you are able to assess your instructional practice will you be able to formulate a plan for growth that will improve the quality of inquiry that you lead within your classrooms.

EQUIP OVERVIEW

Good teachers use many different instructional methods throughout a day, a week, and a year. EQUIP is not designed for all situations; it specifically focuses on the factors associated with the quality of inquiry-based instruction being facilitated by teachers, not with other methods that may be used in the classroom. Our advice is to use EQUIP to obtain a solid point of reference that honestly reflects what you are doing in the classroom, and then develop a plan to raise the level of performance. EQUIP addresses indicators that relate to five specific factors that support inquiry-based teaching and learning:

- Time Usage
- Instruction
- Discourse
- Assessment
- Curriculum

Several indicators associated with each factor are first evaluated, and then a holistic score for each of the last four factors is determined. This holistic score is not necessarily the mean of the indicators, but instead should reflect the essence of the lesson relative to that factor. The complete EQUIP instrument is found in the Appendix or can be downloaded from www.clemson.edu/iim. In this chapter, after a description of the first parts of the instrument, we focus our attention on Instruction, Discourse, Assessment, and Curriculum.

The first three sections of EQUIP are intended mainly for researchers and thus are addressed only briefly here before we move to the critical sections for practicing teachers. Those who wish to be trained on the complete use of the instrument may wish to contact us. Section I contains basic demographic information as well as descriptive lesson information such as objectives and standards. Section II is used to rate five-minute snapshots on several issues such as student attention and cognitive level. Section III is used for field notes that teachers may or may not want to use, depending on their goals for individual growth. The column concerning "Classroom Notes of Observation" is for the evaluator to indicate as objectively as possible what has transpired in the class. The "Comments" column is for the evaluator to express her/his interpretation of what is going on; consequently it is more subjective.

Sections IV-VIII of EQUIP are critical for all assessments conducted. Specifically, they require input of data to assess indicators related to important factors of inquiry-based instruction. In these five sections, the evaluator determines the level of inquiry demonstrated on several indicators associated with the relevant factor. We have designated four possible performance levels for each indicator: Pre-Inquiry (Level 1), Developing Inquiry (Level 2), Proficient Inquiry (Level 3), and Exemplary Inquiry (Level 4). The rubrics provided with each indicator present a description of each level for every indicator. These not only guide the assessment for the indicators for an observation, but also give a target for teachers to shoot for individually or collectively. If your own goal is a high-level inquiry experience, then you should strive for at least Level 3. We advise you and other teachers with whom you work to avoid becoming defensive about the ratings; it is more important to understand why a score falls into a specific level and what can be done to advance to a higher level in the future.

Once you have a benchmark measurement, then working alone or with a team of teachers you can begin to chart your growth and target areas where you wish to improve (see Chapter 7). This helps to move from the "I know it when I see it" to an understanding of the specific aspects of a lesson that make inquiry effective. The insights gained when using EQUIP can provide a foundation for developing a plan that will ultimately improve instruction and student learning.

There are several ways to use the EQUIP to assess a particular class:

- Teachers can use it to reflect back upon a lesson (most convenient but least valuable and most subjective).

- Teachers can videotape a lesson and then go back and complete the protocol either alone or with peers during a replay of the lesson.

- Teachers can complete the instrument while observing another's class.

- An instructional coach or curriculum coordinator can use it to guide conversations with a teacher or team of teachers.

The selection of which strategy to use depends upon the setting and the availability of time and people. We recommend, however, that you try to use the third or fourth options listed above, as we have found that involving others usually leads to a healthy dialogue and provides insights that teachers often miss when viewing their own classroom practice without another set of eyes to assist them. For maximum benefit, and particularly for research purposes, training on EQUIP is essential. Nevertheless, even without training, teachers can gain important information about their practice through its use by understanding the factors and the indicators for these factors that are associated with inquiry-based instruction.

In the following pages, we discuss the factors of Instruction, Discourse, Assessment, and Curriculum in more depth as we illustrate the application of EQUIP. Again, the indicators for these factors are all assessed at the end of the observational period. We provide a science and math example to demonstrate how we use EQUIP.

The science example comes from a physical science lesson framed by the essential question *"What factors affect the motion of an object?"* In the observation from which the example is drawn, the teacher provided teams of 3 or 4 students with mousetrap racer kits and challenged them to create a mousetrap racer that would go 5 meters the fastest, but would stop before it had traveled 6 meters. This competition incorporated process skills (e.g., asking good scientific questions, collecting meaningful data, analyzing results,) and conceptual ideas (e.g., speed, motion, force, conservation of energy) from science, math, and engineering.

The math example is based on a problem entitled "Where Should It Be?" In this problem, a fast food chain sets up five restaurants along a highway at mile markers 2, 4, 16, 28, and 50. There are five trucks, one going to each of the five restaurants (a single truck cannot service more than one restaurant on a trip.) The problem is to determine where a distribution center should be located so that the total number of miles driven is minimized. After this problem is solved, a sixth store is added at mile marker 80. The question remains the same. Students are then expected to generalize and in some way demonstrate a proof of their results. The purpose of the problem is to have students determine and learn important characteristics of measures of center, as well as to refine their process skills, including, among others, problem solving, determining an appropriate method, organizing information, communicating, and mathematical reasoning.

INSTRUCTION

Figure 4-1 shows two of five indicators that comprise the factor of Instruction. Below the figure, we discuss our ratings for our sample science and math observations described above. Because the indicators are associated with the same factor, there are connections among them. However, these connections are not absolute; there are sufficient distinctions among the indicators so that the levels often vary considerably even within the same factor.

Figure 4-1: Sample of Instructional Indicators associated with inquiry-based instruction

IV. Instructional Indicators				
Indicator Measured	Pre-Inquiry (Level 1)	Developing Inquiry (Level 2)	Proficient Inquiry (Level 3)	Exemplary Inquiry (Level 4)
Instructional Strategies	Teacher predominantly lectured to cover content.	Teacher frequently lectured and/or used demonstrations to explain content. Activities were verification only.	Teacher occasionally lectured, but students were engaged in activities that helped develop conceptual understanding.	Teacher occasionally lectured, but students were engaged in investigations that promoted strong conceptual understanding.
Order of Instruction	Teacher explained concepts. Students either did not explore concepts or did so only after explanation.	Teacher asked students to explore concept before receiving explanation. Teacher explained.	Teacher asked students to explore before explanation. Teacher and students explained.	Teacher asked students to explore concept before explanation occurred. Though perhaps prompted by the teacher, students provided the explanation.

Science

Because the teacher provided the vehicle assembly instructions before students had sufficient time to think through their own creation and because she stopped and lectured about the terminology associated with motion, the *Instructional Strategies* earned a Level 2 inquiry rating. Had the teacher provided more opportunities for input of student ideas throughout the investigation, then the quality of the inquiry would have been at least Level 3.

The teacher did, however, achieve a Level 3 inquiry rating for *Order of Instruction* because the lesson engaged the students in exploring concepts before the teacher explained them, and students were involved in explaining their conceptual ideas to the teacher and their peers.

Math

This class was rated Level 3 on *Instructional Strategies*. Though the Engage part of the lesson was minimal, the teacher then presented the problem and gave the students, who were working in groups of three, a considerable amount of time to explore the problem and develop the ideas for themselves. She gave them several prompts to challenge their thinking and to push them toward the underlying ideas. It did not reach Level 4 because the teacher used lecture rather than the investigation to promote conceptual understanding. However, the lesson was above Level 2 because the students were discovering the ideas for themselves.

In regard to *Order of Instruction*, the instruction earned a Level 2 rating. After a solid exploration during which students were developing the conceptual ideas, the teacher lectured the class with only minimal participation by the students. She told them what they should have found and what the underlying principles were, and then provided an informal proof of these principles. To earn a higher rating, she should have given the students a much greater role in this explanation, guiding them as necessary to assist them.

DISCOURSE

Discourse measures the classroom climate and interactions relating to inquiry instruction and learning. Two of five indicators associated with this factor are shown in Figure 4-2.

Figure 4-2: Sample of Discourse Indicators associated with inquiry-based instruction

V. Discourse Indicators				
Indicator Measured	Pre-Inquiry (Level 1)	Developing Inquiry (Level 2)	Proficient Inquiry (Level 3)	Exemplary Inquiry (Level 4)
Questioning Level	Questioning rarely challenged students above the remembering level.	Questioning rarely challenged students above the understanding level.	Questioning challenged students up to application or analysis levels.	Questioning challenged students at various levels, including at the analysis level or higher; level was varied to scaffold learning.
Classroom Interaction	Teacher accepted answers, correcting when necessary, but rarely followed-up with further probing.	Teacher or another student occasionally followed-up student response with further low-level probe.	Teacher or another student often followed-up response with engaging probe that required student to justify reasoning or evidence.	Teacher consistently and effectively facilitated rich classroom dialogue where evidence, assumptions, and reasoning were challenged by teacher or other students.

Science

As the lesson progressed, the teacher provided challenging, higher-level questions (e.g., How did your results compare with those from other groups?) as students presented their findings, which resulted in a Level 3 inquiry rating for *Questioning Level*. However, once students responded to the higher-level questions, the quality of the interactions dropped as the teacher followed-up responses with only low-level probes (e.g., How did you find the second point on the graph?). This resulted in a rating of Level 2 for *Classroom Interaction*. The teacher could raise this score by following-up student responses with more thought-provoking questions such as, "Why was the slope calculated by group 2 larger than the slope calculated by group 1? What does that slope tell us?"

Math

Though the prompts given for the problem were challenging and had the potential to develop deep understanding, the *Questioning Level* earned a Level 2 rating. The teacher asked questions such as "What would happen if the original five mile markers were different?" but did not go beyond expecting the students to state simply and directly that the distribution center should be located at the middle mile marker. The teacher explained the concepts at deeper levels, not involving the students in significant discourse after the exploration. It was, however, above Level 1 because she did expect them to think and not simply remember what they had found. *Classroom Interaction* was rated at Level 1. She asked questions that had short, direct answers and did not follow them up with probing questions or asking other students to respond.

ASSESSMENT

Five indicators are used to measure the Assessment factor relating to instructional practice. Two of the indicators are shown in Figure 4-3.

Figure 4-3: Sample of Assessment Indicators associated with inquiry-based instruction

VI. Assessment Indicators				
Indicator Measured	Pre-Inquiry (Level 1)	Developing Inquiry (Level 2)	Proficient Inquiry (Level 3)	Exemplary Inquiry (Level 4)
Prior Knowledge	Teacher did not assess student prior knowledge.	Teacher assessed student prior knowledge but did not modify instruction based on this knowledge.	Teacher assessed student prior knowledge and then partially modified instruction based on this knowledge.	Teacher assessed student prior knowledge and then modified instruction based on this knowledge.
Conceptual Development	Teacher encouraged learning by memorization and repetition.	Teacher encouraged product- or answer-focused learning activities that lacked critical thinking.	Teacher encouraged process-focused learning activities that required critical thinking.	Teacher encouraged process-focused learning activities that involved critical thinking that connected learning with other concepts.

Science

Because the teacher did not attempt to assess or take into consideration the prior knowledge students possessed, the lesson earned a Level 1 inquiry rating for *Prior Knowledge*. A short pre-test, a KWL chart, or even a discussion concerning what students already knew may have revealed strengths or, on the other hand, some misconceptions regarding motion that should be addressed. The teacher also fell short on *Conceptual Development*. When formative assessments are implemented throughout the lesson, student learning increases. By making the lesson more prescribed than necessary, critical thinking was minimized. This resulted in a Level 2 rating for this indicator. When students are challenged to defend their solutions to scientific questions, a Level 3 or 4 rating is appropriate.

Math

The math lesson for our example received the same ratings as the science lesson. *Prior Knowledge* was rated at Level 1 as the teacher did not ask questions concerning what students knew about the characteristics of center or did not have them make predictions about the answer. We wondered whether she might have done this earlier, but when we talked with her after the class, we found that she had not done so. *Conceptual Development* earned a Level 2 rating. This was a difficult determination because we could not easily tell whether the teacher simply wanted students to memorize that the median is the measure of center that minimizes the total distance to the data points, which would have earned a Level 1 score, or expected the students to understand the result because of the way in which the ideas had been developed. Because of the strong exploration that preceded the explanation of the underlying concepts, we decided to rate the lesson at Level 2. In fact, had the explanation involved the students more in using their exploration to determine the underlying concepts, the lesson could have earned a Level 3 rating.

CURRICULUM

The EQUIP includes four indicators associated with various Curriculum issues related to inquiry instruction. These indicators are tied directly to what is experienced by students, not what appears in a text or notes. *Organizing and Recording Information* is one of several areas in which teachers can provide students with different levels of scaffolding—thus differentiating instruction. The goal is to challenge all students to their highest level while not overly frustrating anyone. For instance, one student with a learning disability may need the structure that a graphic organizer provides, whereas an ESL student may need more visuals to help decode the language barriers. We should always strive to help students progress to a level where less direct assistance is needed. By doing so, we will have encouraged and helped to develop habits of lifelong learning. To earn Level 4 on this and other indicators, teachers should consider the various needs of *all* students in their class. Two of the Curriculum indicators, *Integration of Content and Investigation* and *Organizing and Recording Information*, are displayed in Figure 4-4.

Figure 4-4: Sample of Curriculum Indicators associated with inquiry-based instruction

VII. Curriculum Indicators				
Indicator Measured	Pre-Inquiry (Level 1)	Developing Inquiry (Level 2)	Proficient Inquiry (Level 3)	Exemplary Inquiry (Level 4)
Integration of Content & Investigation	Lesson either content-focused or activity-focused but not both.	Lesson provided poor integration of content with activity or investigation.	Lesson incorporated student investigation that linked well with content.	Lesson seamlessly integrated the content and the student investigation.
Organizing & Recording Information	Students organized and recorded information in prescriptive ways.	Students had only minor input as to how to organize and record information.	Students regularly organized and recorded information in non-prescriptive ways.	Students organized and recorded information in non-prescriptive ways that allowed them to effectively communicate their learning.

Science

The *Integration of Content and Investigation* earned a Level 3 inquiry rating because the investigation almost continually integrated concepts such as speed vs. time graphs and conservation of energy into the student investigations. *Organizing and Recording Information* was scored at Level 2 because the teacher provided little opportunity for the students to determine how the data should be collected and organized. When data sheets are provided with the headings and axes already labeled, which is what happened during this observation, students are deprived of a rich opportunity to think about how to collect, organize, and convey meaning from the data. By having the opportunity to organize and record information as they see fit, students think more deeply and more critically about the concepts being investigated (e.g., how many trials are needed? Is speed the independent or dependent variable, and why?). Had the teacher provided this opportunity, the rating for this indicator would have risen to a Level 3 or 4.

Math

The lesson had an excellent activity and was targeted at important mathematical content. However, these two facets of the class were not integrated well, as, after the investigation, the teacher explained the concepts without much student input and did not clearly guide the students in mastering the underlying ideas based upon their findings. Consequently, the lesson earned a Level

2 rating on *Integration of Content and Investigation*. The class earned a Level 3 rating on *Organizing & Recording Information*. During the exploration, the teacher encouraged the students to organize their data in some logical manner and to make sure they had records of all of their attempts, but did not tell them how to do this. It fell short of a Level 4 because the students did not use their data to communicate to the teacher or other students, either in oral or written form, what they had learned.

IMPROVING QUALITY OF INQUIRY TEACHING

After each of the indicators associated with the five factors (the four just discussed plus Time Usage) has been assessed, in Section VIII of EQUIP an overall, or holistic, rating is determined for each factor. Again, this holistic rating is not necessarily the mean of the indicators, but is the Level that best captures the essence of the lesson. Though it may seem that approaching the rating this way would make this section overly subjective, we have found that our inter-rater reliability, or consistency between different raters, is quite high.

Once the instrument has been completed and the current state of inquiry instruction is established, the next step is to improve the quality of inquiry. Though establishing the benchmark may bring about some change just by having specific aspects of instructional practice brought to the teacher's attention, the goal is to become more intentional and explicit by developing an action plan of next steps. It is normal to desire to improve everything that ails our instruction all at once. However, such a course of action often leads to frustration and undue anxiety; effective change is usually incremental.

Our recommendation is for the teacher to focus on one specific indicator (not even an entire factor) that she wishes to improve upon during the next lesson or unit of study. Once the desired growth has been achieved, then it is time to tackle another indicator. After four indicators relating to inquiry instruction have been improved, perhaps one from each of the factors Instruction, Discourse, Assessment, and Curriculum, the teacher should strive to maintain that level of performance before undertaking more improvements. If teachers work together and note common areas for growth, it may make sense to work on certain indicators together. This shared approach provides a support structure to exchange thoughts and ideas. Chapter 7 provides more specifics about developing a plan for improvement.

If current practice falls largely in Level 1, then it makes sense to begin reading about constructivist approaches to learning and inquiry-based methods of teaching, looking for examples of lessons and instruction. Many articles from NCTM and NSTA journals (e.g. *The Science Teacher, The Mathematics Teacher*), along with journals from other professional organizations, provide these, along with many innovative ideas that can be of immense value to teachers who wish to modify their practice. Also, teachers may seek out any one of many professional development institutes that provide opportunities to experience inquiry learning firsthand. Generally, a Level 2 performance suggests that a teacher is familiar with getting students engaged and active, but the lessons tend to be more prescriptive, with students having only limited opportunities to develop the ideas for themselves. Additionally, instruction is still heavily teacher-focused. At Level 3, the teacher has demonstrated a student-centered inquiry-learning environment that actively engages students in investigations, questioning, and explanations. The role of the teacher remains vital (as it does at all levels), but she now functions more as a facilitator who scaffolds learning experiences than as a giver of facts and knowledge.

We do not expect that any one lesson would merit a Level 4 for all indicators or even for all factors. In fact, we have yet to see such a lesson, and we have seen some amazing lessons. The point is not to make every instructional moment a Level 3 or higher; rather, the goal is to help you become more intentional about your practice. By making you aware of what high quality inquiry practice entails, we believe you will be more likely to implement it successfully when it is your desired instructional approach.

We hope that the EQUIP provides you, the teacher, with a concrete way to reflect on your own teaching practice as you strive to lead inquiry-based learning experiences in your classroom. Inquiry instruction is challenging to implement well, but, when done effectively, learning is clearly evident with *all* students and at *all* ability levels.

ENDNOTES

1.   Marshall, J. C.; Horton, R. M., The relationship of teacher facilitated inquiry-based instruction to student higher-order thinking. *School Science and Mathematics* In Review.

2.   Donovan, M. S.; Bransford, J. D., *How students learn: history, mathematics, and science in the classroom.* National Academies Press: Washington, DC, 2005.

3.   Llewellyn, D., *Inquiry within: Implementing inquiry-based science standards.* Corwin Press: Thousand Oaks, CA, 2002.

4.   National Research Council, *Inquiry and the national science education standards: A guide for teaching and learning.* National Academies Press: Washington, DC, 2000.

5.   Marshall, J. C.; Smart, J.; Horton, R. M., The Design and Validation of EQUIP: An Instrument to Assess Inquiry-Based Instruction. *International Journal of Science and Mathematics Education* In Press.

6.   Marshall, J. C.; Horton, B.; White, C., EQUIPping teachers: A protocol to guide and improve inquiry-based instruction. *The Science Teacher* 2009, 76, (4), 46-53.

7.   National Research Council, *National science education standards.* National Academies Press: Washington, DC, 1996.

8.   Marshall, J. C.; Horton, B.; Edmondson, E. 4E x 2 Instructional Model *Periodical* [Online], 2007. www.clemson.edu/iim (accessed May 15, 2009).

9.   Marshall, J. C.; Horton, B.; Smart, J., 4E x 2 Instructional Model: Uniting three learning constructs to improve praxis in science and mathematics classrooms. *Journal of Science Teacher Education* In Press.

CHAPTER 5

MEASURING STUDENT ACHIEVEMENT

The ultimate measure in education is whether what we do as professionals results in student learning and achievement. Without question this is one of the most difficult aspects of educational research because the variables involved in going from teacher practice to student achievement are staggering. Furthermore, the instruments we use to measure student achievement assess only a subset of a student's total knowledge and skills. Perhaps, in a tightly controlled lab setting, student performance could be measured with great accuracy and fairness, but even then aspects such as social interactions, retention of knowledge over time, and transference of knowledge to new situations are omitted. Thus, we need to strive for a balance between contrived lab settings and the real, unobstructed world of learning so that we can understand the learners' strengths and weaknesses and determine the growth resulting from teaching.

In this chapter, we discuss some ideas on assessing student growth. This chapter may be most relevant for those in charge of assessing the school or district's growth in student achievement, but classroom teachers can benefit from the chapter by investigating some of the more global issues of assessment that are also directly relevant to them.

To frame our discussion on assessing student achievement, we share how we have striven to evaluate our professional development institutes for science and mathematics teachers that are designed to increase the quantity and quality of inquiry used in the classroom. Specifically, we wanted to know how teacher participation in this program influences student achievement. In the section that follows, we discuss the different types of assessments that we could consider to help us meet our needs.

OVERVIEW OF ASSESSMENTS

There are many options available to measure student achievement. Each carries with it strengths and limitations. Common assessments that are used to measure student achievement include teacher-made tests, departmental or district tests, and state or national examinations. In the paragraphs that follow, we explore each of these, often referring to the context of our professional development institute.

Teacher-Made Tests

Teacher-made tests are rarely subjected to studies of reliability and validity and are largely subjective even if they are constructed as objective tests. How should items be asked? How should they be weighted? What percent of the test should concern each objective? How should partial credit be awarded? All of these are subjective, left to the discretion of the teacher.

Nevertheless, teacher-made tests can also be one of the best indicators of the progress that has occurred in the classroom. Specifically, the classroom teacher knows better than anyone which targeted goals and objectives received the most attention. When teachers diverge from the intended path, taking advantage of teachable moments, they need the flexibility to assess what has been taught. However, challenges arise. One challenge is whether or not the assessments used really measure student knowledge relative to the objectives addressed in class, whether originally intended or not. Another is that these tests typically do not provide information as to whether one form of instruction works better than another. Nevertheless, they do provide important information.

As teachers construct and use their own tests, or even those supplied by the textbook companies or other publishers, we encourage them to focus on the verbs in their objectives and standards. For example, consider the math standard "Represent and analyze mathematical situations and structures using algebraic symbols" (NCTM, 2000, p. 296). We observed a teacher who addressed this standard by presenting a real-world scenario in class, asking students to explore the scenario and describe it in their own words, represent it graphically, and then determine and interpret an algebraic model that described the situation. We found the instruction to be outstanding. However, when we studied the summative assessment instrument the teacher used, we found only problems that demonstrated whether students could remember what they had done in class, problems that asked students to graph and solve equations similar in form to the model created in the lesson. The items functioned more as exercises than as problems. Instead, we believe that she should have presented a new scenario to the students and asked them to explore, describe and analyze this scenario and then determine and interpret an algebraic model for it. In short, her teaching targeted higher-level learning, but her assessment did not. If the objective is for students to represent and analyze a situation, then not only does the teaching need to guide students in learning how to do so, but the assessment must determine if they can do so.

Though aligning assessment with instruction may seem obvious, it is often difficult to implement. From our own experiences visiting hundreds of classrooms over the years, we have found that no matter the depth of the objectives, the formal assessments tend to be easy-to-score instruments that assess only shallow understanding and efficiency in procedures, symbolic manipulation, and/or memorization of facts. This is, in our opinion, one of the major impediments to effective teaching and, indeed, to the effective use of inquiry. We as teachers are accustomed to assessments that target efficiency in procedure and recitation of facts, which are much simpler to evaluate and require less time. However, because students quickly learn what counts, assessments of this nature diminish the depth of learning and understanding for which we strive. To be most effective, the distinction between instruction and assessment should be nearly invisible; instruction and assessment should be fully aligned; and in fact, teachers, as we have argued in our instructional model, should be assessing as they are instructing. Summative assessments should not be dramatically different from—and may at times be identical to—the formative assessments that are used during instruction.

Despite the difficulties inherent in teacher-constructed assessments, they can still be extremely effective in determining what students have learned as long as teachers create them in a conscientious, intentional way. Teachers can compare how their students performed to what they have done on a pre-assessment and to how students have done in previous years, and they can share and compare results with other teachers. These are all valuable and important. However, even when teacher-developed tests are strong, they are still of limited use for evaluating programs such as our professional development institute. To evaluate the program's effectiveness, we needed a more widely used and validated assessment. Specifically, we needed to be measuring student results on common objectives and standards for all the participants and comparing these results with those from non-participants.

Departmental and District Tests

Tests that are created by departments or districts try to seek an objective and valid way to align the performance of students in various classes within the department or throughout the district. These have several advantages because they can provide a barometer that allows comparisons of student performance across classes within a building. During planning meetings, results from these tests provide an opportunity to look at general trends in the performance of students. For instance, the results may show that students generally understand how to calculate or answer specific problems related to a key concept such as density, but further analysis may reveal that learning is shallow and perfunctory. Teams can then begin to target strategies that allow instruction to improve during the next iteration. Specific formative assessments conducted during units of study allow instructional plans to be revised so that they better align with student needs.

There are, of course, drawbacks to departmental and district tests. Teachers will likely feel strong pressure to teach to the test, rather than address a teachable moment that veers away from the intended instruction. Particularly when it comes to inquiry-based teaching and learning, it takes an immense amount of faith to have confidence that students who learn at the deeper levels that inquiry promotes will perform just as well as students who were prepared more directly for the assessment. This temptation, to teach for a specific assessment rather than for deeper learning, a temptation that is particularly strong in this era of accountability, is difficult to overcome, especially for those who are trying a method that is new to them and may take them months or even years to master. It is far easier to succumb and simply use a "teaching as telling" model to prepare students for the test. Ultimately, though, teachers' decisions should be based upon what is best to maximize student learning.

Other issues arise as well. If the results of specific instruments have important repercussions, then it becomes more imperative to ensure that the instruments are reliable and valid. Have people with expertise in assessment been involved with their creation? Instruments that have not been scientifically created and tested should not be used for high-stakes decisions (and even those that have should not be the sole measures of these decisions). This, of course, requires more time and often more money, two quantities often in short supply.

Furthermore, with departmental and district tests, teachers may feel that they, not the students, are the ones being assessed. How do their students stack up again other teachers' students? Are the comparisons fair? In a more positive light, teachers can sometimes use these tests to ensure that they themselves have the requisite content knowledge to teach the material effectively and to gain a better understanding of which ideas should be emphasized and which ones may not be as critical.

In regard to our efforts to evaluate our program, we had to look elsewhere. The district simply did not have tests that aligned with our objectives, though they are working on them now. Once available, then we will have a different challenge: figuring out how to use the district tests to compare the achievement of our participants' students with the achievement of non-participants' students. Though overall comparisons may be easy, there are many confounding concerns, such as previous performance of the schools, the level of the students coming in, and the prior experiences of the teachers. District tests would be helpful; our point here is that assessing the effectiveness of a program can still be problematic.

State and National Tests

One of the challenges we face is that many districts use end-of-year tests as the primary measure of student achievement. While these tests show trends among schools, districts, states, and nations, they do not necessarily provide a valid assessment of student growth because there are so many factors that can confound the results. First, pretests, which can be expensive and time consuming, are usually not available to provide specific information on growth during a given year. Second, no demographic data is used to equate the groups. Third, these tests necessarily provide information on only a subset of the learning that has taken place; they cannot measure all that was taught. Fourth, they are not always aligned to the standards being taught. Fifth, they do not always provide detailed information about student performance, but rather an overall rating. Finally, many intervening events (e.g., illnesses, school disruptions, historical events) can either interfere with learning or influence learning outside of the classroom. In terms of assessing a program such as ours, they are even more problematic than district tests.

Despite these challenges, such tests can provide valuable information. State and national tests are beneficial for seeing trends of student performance at the school, district, and state levels. For large populations such as large districts or states, it is possible to make claims about student achievement relative to the performance of students in prior years, and, in some cases, to other schools. However, we should always keep in mind that as the sample size decreases to the class level, it is more difficult to make accurate claims that compare student performance. As mentioned earlier, there are just too many intervening variables. Teachers can still get a sense of how their students have done compared with what their students have done in the past and with what other students in their school have done, but they should recognize that these are not scientifically sound interpretations.

As classrooms have moved to performance-based assessments for learning, norm-referenced tests have begun to lose their value. Instead of comparing students to other students, the emphasis today is on criterion-referenced instruments in which students must meet a pre-determined level of performance to be considered proficient on a standard. Thus, we have seen a rise in popularity of tests like the NAEP (National Assessment of Educational Progress)[1] that sets clear benchmarks for students, schools, and states to achieve. One positive aspect of this move toward criterion-referenced instruments is that rather than students competing against each other, it is to their advantage to learn from each other cooperatively, helping all parties attain proficiency.

Though tests such as NAEP provide valuable information, they could not help us determine if our professional development program improves student achievement. Thus, we faced a dilemma common in education. On one hand, assessment instruments commonly used in school systems were not necessarily aligned to measure the particular academic goals we wished to achieve. As a result, the use of a state assessment, or traditional standardized test, would introduce "noise" into the evaluation effort that would make it difficult or impossible to identify whether there was a meaningful academic effect. On the other hand, introducing a well-targeted assessment would be intrusive. Schools and teachers already feel students are over-tested, so taking away instructional time was not a winning option. Furthermore, we recognized that students might lack any meaningful incentive to offer their best performance on an instrument that was not part of their instructional program.

MAP TEST OVERVIEW

Our solution was to use MAP (Measure of Academic Progress). Fortunately, the district with whom we were working had already adopted MAP, and we found that the MAP test had several strengths for what we wanted to achieve:

- MAP is aligned to our state standards in mathematics and science, which minimizes the noise introduced when the assessment is not well aligned to the learning objectives. In addition, MAP is used throughout our state, which permits the comparison of results from the instrument across districts. Predictive validity between the MAP assessment and other state assessments is generally quite high[2,3]. MAP is also used throughout the country, giving us, if we are careful, additional means to assess our program. We discuss this more below.

- MAP is an adaptive assessment. Because of this, no two students take the same form of the assessment. This means, when evaluating group results, that MAP provides a broader, more robust sample of the domain than can be generated from a single fixed form assessment administered to a group of students[4]. It also makes it easier to study sub-domains of a content area, because a group of several hundred students provides a sufficient number of item responses on a large array of items to produce rich, meaningful results. Also, because of the large number of items from which MAP draws, teachers cannot simply "teach to the test."

- MAP uses a Rasch-scaled[5] item pool rather than a scaled test form. For example, the approximately 5,000 active items in the MAP mathematics item pool are all calibrated to a single cross-grade Rasch-based scale. This calibrated item pool becomes the "parent" of all tests created from the pool. Thus one can flag portions of a particular test's item pool for analysis and, as long as the items selected adequately cover the scale's range, compare the results of this analysis to other domains and populations.

- MAP assesses students at whatever grade level they are working, not necessarily at the grade they are in, and offers information on individual student change in performance[6]. This facilitates more accurate measurement of student growth across time.

POWER OF MAP

The evaluation design that incorporates the MAP test allowed us to make several comparisons, since we were able to control for several factors—thus, allowing us to gain information about the effectiveness of our program. Specifically,

- Pre-post measurement of the students taught by teachers in our professional development institutes allowed us to measure growth during the current academic year. This growth was then compared to the growth of students with non-participating teachers in the district and to students in a Virtual Comparison Group, which is discussed more fully below.

- Pre-post measures for the students of participating teachers from the year prior to intervention provided a solid baseline of expected growth. We then compared growth during the intervention year with this previous growth. Though by itself not conclusive, greater growth during the intervention year would give some indication that our efforts were successful.

- Pre-post measurement of the students of non-participating educators helped control for a school or district effect and the influence that interventions or changes within our participating schools might have had on the growth of students during the study period. This helped us determine whether any reported gains were the result of our intervention or other district programs.

- The continued collection of data for two years after completion of the program made it possible to determine whether any effect found for the program persisted. It also permitted us to investigate whether there was a "J-curve" effect associated with our intervention. The J-curve phenomenon suggests that as a new reform is implemented that a lag, and even a slight drop, can occur until the teacher becomes comfortable with the changes[7]. If the reform is effective, student outcomes will improve in the long run, provided that sufficient time is allowed to overcome a possible J-curve effect[8].

- Perhaps most importantly, the use of Virtual Comparison Groups introduced a control for effects that might be a product of variance in the student cohorts. The use of matched student groups helped assure that any gains reported by the program were linked to improvements in instruction and not a product of differences among the students taught prior to and after the intervention. This is further explained below.

The criteria for creating the Virtual Comparison Group are as follows:

1. Each student in the study group is matched with up to 51 students who serve as virtual comparisons. Students who cannot be matched with at least 21 students are excluded from the analysis.
2. Selected VCG students must have an overall scale score within one point of their study group student on the pretest measure.
3. Each VCG student must have been tested within +/- 7 days of the study group student.
4. Each VCG student must come from a school with a Free and Reduced Lunch participation rate that is within 5% of the study group student's school.
5. Each VCG student must come from a school with the same urban/rural designation in the National Center for Educational Statistics Common Core of Data as the study group student's school.
6. Each VCG student must have the same gender and ethnic designation as the study group student.

The employment of Virtual Comparison Groups in evaluation studies can be a robust and non-intrusive option for studying the effectiveness of school or university programs that are aimed at improving student learning. However, we fully recognize that the opportunity for such comparisons is not realistic in all settings.

Our hope is that more and more districts and states will recognize the difficulties inherent in measuring growth in student achievement and the effectiveness of programs. By moving toward the use of tests that are widely available and have the flexibility to make the comparisons we have described, particularly with Virtual Comparison Groups, not only will we have better evidence upon which to make educational decisions, but perhaps we can even reduce the number of days that students lose instructional time by taking high-stakes tests and reduce the amount of money spent on test construction, evaluation, and security.

ENDNOTES

1.   National Assessment of Educational Progress *NAEP 2000 science assessment results released*; NCES 2002-452; United States Department of Education, : Jessup, MD, 2002.

2.   Northwest Evaluation Association, *NWEA Reliability and Validity Estimates: Achievement Level Tests and Measures of Academic Progress.* Author: Lake Oswego, OR, 2005.

3.   Cronin, J.; Kingsbury, G. G.; Dahlin, M.; Adkins, D.; Bowe, B., Alternate methodologies for estimating state standards on a widely-used computerized adaptive test. In *National Council on Measurement in Education*, Chicago, IL, 2007.

4.   Northwest Evaluation Association, *Technical manual.* Author: Lake Oswego, OR, 2003.

5.   Smith, E. V., Evidence for the reliability of measures and validity of measure interpretation: A Rasch measurement perspective. *Journal of Applied Measurement* 2001, 2, (3), 281-311.

6.   Northwest Evaluation Association, *RIT scale norms.* Author: Lake Oswego, OR, 2005.

7.   Erb, T. O.; Stevenson, C., Middle school reforms throw a J-Curve: Don't strike out. *Middle School Journal* 1999, 45-47.

8.   Yore, L.; Anderson, J.; Shymansky, J., Sensing the impact of elementary school science reform: A study of stakeholder perceptions of implementation, constructivist strategies, and school-home collaboration. *Journal of Science Teacher Education* 2005, 16, (1), 65-88.

CHAPTER 6

MANAGING AN INQUIRY CLASSROOM EFFECTIVELY

One of the greatest fears for teachers in implementing inquiry-based instruction is the fear of losing control—control of instruction, control of students, control of the class. Unless teachers address this fear, they will likely continue to rationalize their unwillingness to implement inquiry instruction instead of asking what is best for students and then working to achieve that goal. The fear is real. After all, management issues are the main reason that people leave the teaching profession[1]. With knowledge and effort, however, this fear can be addressed and overcome. This chapter gives suggestions and guidance so that you will be able to manage your inquiry-based classroom effectively. Some of our suggestions are relevant to effective management in general, but many are unique to inquiry-based instruction.

We commonly hear teachers say that inquiry works with students of high ability but not students of lower ability, primarily because of behavioral issues. Yet, we also hear other teachers say that inquiry techniques work best with students of lower ability because inquiry provides a way to engage these students in learning, some for the first time. So why the contradiction?

We have found teachers' receptivity to inquiry instruction rests, at least in part, on their success, or lack thereof, in managing the classroom effectively. Classroom management is undoubtedly one of the most critical aspects associated with effective instruction and learning. Poor management can destroy any chance for meaningful learning. However, the converse is not necessarily true. Strong management is a necessity for effective pedagogy to occur, but it does not in and of itself ensure that powerful learning will transpire. Though behavior management is certainly the most obvious form of classroom management and the area that breeds the most fear for teachers, other areas of classroom management exist. In this chapter we provide suggestions on managing behavior, but also on other forms of management that play a significant role in determining how successful the class is.

BUILDING A SOLID PRESENCE

Any two teachers will be perceived differently even if they say the same thing to a class of students. One will likely have a greater command of the classroom interactions than the other because of her presence. A commanding presence carries a firmness, a fairness, a confidence, and a "withitness" that allow the classroom to operate safely and respectfully—thus allowing and encouraging learning to take place. Though these qualities tend to improve with time and experience, they can also be learned so that novice teachers can establish a commanding presence and quickly pass the "tests" that their students will inevitably send their way. To be clear, firmness is not equivalent to meanness. As teachers, we should *never* be mean, but firmness is often necessary. This lesson is often difficult for new teachers—a teacher needs to be the adult in the room, set reasonable boundaries, and expect that everyone live within those boundaries. Fairness strives for equity and impartiality. Treating students with impartiality and equity means addressing the unique needs of each learner, which requires that all are treated with fairness but not necessarily with sameness. Thus, successful teachers avoid playing favorites.

Confidence does not mean cockiness, but rather a self-assurance that gives you comfort and an ease of manner. Possessing a solid content knowledge is one great step in building confidence, perhaps in part because this knowledge also comes with the recognition that no one can ever know everything within the discipline. Confidence also extends beyond content knowledge and includes a sense of knowing yourself, your strengths and limitations, and an acknowledgement that you care about your students and are able to interact with them. "Withitness" is a global understanding of what is transpiring in the class at a given time; this comes more easily to those who are good at multitasking, and the awareness develops when a teacher cares about her students, their learning, and the content that she teaches.

RELATIONSHIPS AND RESPECT

If all learners were the same, we should just plug in a videotape of an excellent teacher each day to do the teaching for us. Yet, we know that the needs, the abilities, and the goals of our students are all unique, so our profession is a personal one that requires us to develop a professional rapport with and understanding of each student that we encounter. Thus, our task as teachers includes facilitating the development of a caring and respectful learning environment.

Many battles are waged because of respect, or a lack of it. But a common mistake is to think that respect is given and earned in the same way. Respect is typically culturally dependent. In some settings, respect is commonly yielded up front—you are respected until you lose it. In other settings, particularly those in which the teacher is not a member of the dominant culture, respect often must be earned. Thus, if you possess little background in cultural understanding of your setting, you will likely be frustrated when students do not bestow you with immediate respect[2]. The first step is to acknowledge the differences and remain patient even when norms or belief systems differ. Even though gaining respect may take more time in some settings than others, there are still things that can be done. Be honest with yourself and with the students and acknowledge to the students that respect may take time, and you are okay with that. In the meantime, however, let the students know that you have general expectations regarding decency and civility that all must adhere to. Students don't have to agree with everyone in the class, but you can expect that they will listen to each other, hear each other out, and find appropriate ways to dissent when appropriate.

SETTING HIGH EXPECTATIONS

Many classes that we have observed have no explicit expectations for students. In such cases, the underlying expectation becomes such that the teacher will teach and the student will learn. The students' effectiveness in mastering what you teach will determine their grades, and all will go on their merry way. Well, we typically do not see the merry ending especially when in many of our classes half or more of the students are failing. For those classes that have high pass rates, you are not off the hook either; you owe it to the students to challenge them and help them increase their knowledge and improve their skills, both in the content area and in their process skills, as the year progresses. The need for high, though attainable, expectations for all students is the underlying message. What do high expectations have to do with management? When expectations are clear and high, students know where they are going, they see how their learning fits into the bigger picture, and they tend to see the relevance for them. This pattern becomes a proactive means to manage student learning. When learning has purpose, behavior problems plummet, and learning becomes more of the focal point.

Expectations can be co-created with students. When students feel they have a voice, they are more likely to engage in learning and will even defend it when scoffed at by peers. One means of setting expectations is to have students set short and long-term goals. Long-term goals may be about their performance in the course. Short-term goals may have to do with what they will try to achieve today. Goal setting has become particularly popular in middle school settings and provides one strategy to narrow the achievement gap. Having students focus on clear goals each day helps them both to organize and prioritize, which are two very difficult things for many students. Encouraging students to set their own goals and determining collectively what are appropriate expectations provides a venue to challenge students and minimize the boredom that plagues many of our students. Many of the "trouble makers" are not malicious, but rather they are bored. Yes, some of these students are also missing some critical content and skills, but the discipline problems are most often a call for help and an avoidance of failure rather than a calculated attempt to sabotage your class.

SPECIFIC CHALLENGES INHERENT TO INQUIRY CLASSROOMS

Building a solid presence, encouraging respect, and setting high expectations are all helpful global proactive management strategies, but there are some classroom management challenges that are specifically inherent to inquiry forms of teaching and learning.

First Day

Unquestionably, Day One is the best opportunity we have to establish the conditions that favor an effective learning environment. Remember we only make one first impression[3]. Within a few minutes students are already making up their mind about whether they will enjoy coming to class, how much they are likely to gain from the class, and what effort they will be putting forth for the rest of the term. Though it may seem daunting, a few specific things will tilt the scales in your favor. First, and we do mean at the very first moment if possible, engage students in a short, but meaningful learning experience—one that requires thought and effort but one for which they can experience success. You may be required to address school policies on Day One, but, if possible, shy away from rules, policies, syllabi, and book checkouts. Remember this is likely all they will hear or have heard all day long. All of those things are important, but they can be gradually addressed during the first week.

For those who insist or are required by their school to cover all the nuts and bolts on Day One, there are some strategies for doing it in a way that can also engage students in learning. One such strategy is to set up a series of learning stations for the first day. This gets the focus off of you as the teacher when nerves tend to be a little high anyway. Learning stations are great time management techniques for these things because there is no reason for the entire class to watch while you pass out books one at a time. An example of learning stations might include a series of five or ten minute rotations where students would accomplish each of the following: 1) check out a text (have students take a book, sign the form that they received the book, record the number of the book, find a few key things in the text), 2) complete an intriguing math problem (to avoid dead time throughout the year, we suggest always having a set of recreational brain teasers on hand that are usually, but not always, tied to the curriculum), 3) take a short test for competency (for example, have them use a triple beam balance to measure the mass of the two provided objects, and record their answers to the hundredth of a gram), 4) pick up a copy of the syllabus and respond to a couple of key questions like "What should you do if you miss a day of class?", 5) complete a personal information sheet (collect name, contact numbers, email, parents' names and numbers, and then have them respond to some general questions that you would like to know), and 6) work as a team (have a task that all can work on that requires students to plan and complete something collaboratively, such as building the tallest free standing tower using 1 foot of tape and 25 straws). The list goes on for possible stations (base several on your learning objectives for the year to assess prior knowledge). You will need about 8-10 stations for a class of 30. The key to successful learning stations is to try to make them about equal in time to complete. If one station is particularly short, then add a short problem for them to work. If they see the learning stations as a sort of scavenger hunt that provides a window into the upcoming year, it is fairly easy to get buy in.

For those who have some flexibility, you can save the learning stations for another day. Instead, get them thinking, doing, and exploring. A feeling of success should be the goal for Day One. You may leave them with a more challenging problem later, but students should not be concerned with failing on their first attempt in your class. We have three specific suggestions: get students questioning (e.g., come up with 10 questions that you have about the world around you), get students observing (e.g., make 10 observations of things around the room), and get students collecting data (e.g., weigh 10 objects without a conventional scale). For the first option, it may not surprise you that students have a difficult time asking good questions. We give our pre-service science teachers 15 minutes to go outside and write 20 good "scientific" questions that they have as they look around campus. Few ever come back with 20 questions. This leads into a great discussion about just asking good questions. In math, we ask our students to come up with a list of questions about each other that they would like to know the answers to, data we can use later to tackle key standards; in short order, they come to realize how difficult it can be to write a good question.

These exercises also point out that we have stifled the natural curiosity that we all have when we are young. Instead, schooling has often converted this natural curiosity into compliance of behavior where students are expected to come and receive what we have to give them without meaningfully engaging in their own learning. The point is for you to engage students in exploring and making sense of the world around them from the very first day. This is the greatest motivator of all.

Change Gradually

As you lead inquiry experiences, remember that your students have not had the same experiences as you. Your transition likely occurred over a significant period of time, so be sensitive to this and provide appropriate scaffolding to help your students transition to what will be for many a new strategy for learning. Additionally, recognize that most do not embrace change at first, so know that it takes time to acclimate to new ideas and new ways of thinking.

The EQUIP observational instrument discussed in Chapter 4 provides a rubric to help you as you improve your proficiency relative to implementation of inquiry-based instruction. If your goal is to be at a Level 3 for a given inquiry investigation but you are beginning at Level 1, then it would be prudent to first build toward Level 2, which tends to be more teacher-directed and prescriptive. Nearly all commercial lessons are written at a Level 2. As students begin to assume more ownership in their learning (e.g., learning how to organize ideas, data, and their thinking in more self-directed ways), then the level of inquiry can be raised to match their new abilities. In other words, you are providing scaffolding not only for yourself, but for your students as well. Even if you are already at Level 2, keep in mind that inquiry will be new for many students, so you will still need to provide transitional experiences for them; beginning the year with Level 3 instruction will likely cause undue frustration.

Managing Cooperative Learning

One of the things that often distinguishes inquiry forms of learning from others is the degree of interaction required among peers. Though inquiry can be done in isolation, learning is often social and better accomplished with cooperative forms of learning. This opportunity to increase knowledge through interpersonal interactions can also present a great challenge. Namely, how do you facilitate such learning without the class resulting in utter chaos? First, you have to realize that student discussion can be a good thing. If silence is your *modus operandi*, you might want to rethink why silence is so important to you, and what you believe it achieves. Compliance and silence do not mean that any learning is occurring—they only ensure that disruptions are minimized. Since silence does not equate to learning, the trick is to make sure that talk is directed positively toward the topic of focus.

Group Size. One important consideration is determining the best group size when you have students work together. The short answer is to use whatever best matches the objectives and has the potential to engage everyone in the group. At times, supplies will dictate the minimum group size. When choice is an option, we have had the best results when groups range from 2-4. In math, groups of two are often appropriate if communication of process is the target. Detailing solutions on mini-marker boards can be alternated, for example, and strategies such as think-pair-share can be readily employed. However, we have found that groups of 3 typically work best for us when students are engaged with true problems—with groups of 4, students tend to work in two pairs rather than as one group. In science, for lab investigations, groups of 2-3 typically work nicely. Once groups get larger, there is a tendency for "tag-a-longs" who are not explicitly involved.

Regardless of the group size, the management on your part requires that you keep things moving at a pace that is brisk enough to promote a sense of urgency on the part of students but slow enough to allow students time to think. Creating this sense of urgency will be discussed more in the section on time usage.

Different strategies, of course, work better for different teachers, but we encourage you to reassign groups frequently. In math, you may want to consider every three weeks or so, but in science we encourage every 6-9 weeks since the length of investigations tend to be a bit longer and supply issues tend to be more complicated. Inevitably, students will at times be assigned to work with those whom they do not get along well, but you can assure them that it is only temporary and they can (and *must*) work it out.

Assessing Group Work. Regardless of the group size, it is vital that individual accountability is weighted more heavily then group performance in the final grade earned on a project or investigation. This allows students to work as teams but requires students to be individually responsible for knowing and understanding. (Cathy Plowden, whom you will meet in Chapter 7, does an outstanding job of having students explore and discuss together, but provide individual explanations of the group's findings.) Facilitating group work that has individual accountability is a proactive means to addressing parent and student concerns about unequal workload receiving similar credit. Many rubrics are available to help with distributing the credit appropriately[4]. Students will benefit by fully understanding the criteria by which they will be assessed, and thus will become more focused on the work at hand[5]. Yes, some students will likely work harder than others in group work, but this is real world learning. As you well know, some teachers work harder than others, and they may get paid the same or even less—sound familiar? So if the grade earned is backed by individual accountability, why should students want to cooperate with group members? Perhaps you can provide an incentive for groups to encourage the success of all members on a given objective. This encourages peer tutoring, reviewing together, and more of a team atmosphere. Also, if the task is appropriate and challenging enough, students will know that it is difficult if not impossible to achieve success in isolation and will thus want to work together[6]. Examples of this include building a mini-solar racer that goes 5 meters in the quickest time, or a solving a math problem that requires many different approaches. By rotating the groups regularly, you also lessen the concerns that someone might have for being "stuck" with someone who appears not to care or won't contribute.

Questioning Techniques

How successfully you facilitate discourse in the class is a question of both classroom management and of effective teaching practices. The type of questions that you ask is directly related to the expectations that you have for students. Ask students questions that challenge them to think deeply. If it is at a point in the lesson where students do not know for sure, then allow them an opportunity to conduct some research before they engage in the discourse. For example, asking students to discuss the factors that they themselves can influence related to global warming will generate rich discussion and deep thinking. Contrast this with questions such as, "What did you get for problem #5?" Questions that lead to one-word responses do not generate meaningful discourse.

When you are reviewing problem sets, a good approach is to post the solutions on the board or overhead and then ask students which problems they had difficulty with or are confused by, and why. Then, discussions can focus both on process issues and on clarifying concepts where confusion exists. The goal is to improve thinking in areas where the greatest challenges exist, not just to treat everything as equal and lower level. The EQUIP rubric discussed in Chapter 4 and in the Appendix provides an entire section on things to consider when leading questioning and discourse in an inquiry classroom.

Employing wait time and having all students engaged in the discourse are also critical, and these are things that, with practice, everyone can do. When you ask questions, in addition to making sure that you include many deeper level probes as described above, wait for approximately 5 seconds (which will seem like an eternity if you have not practiced this before) and then call on someone[7]. The wait time should be dependent on the complexity of the question that you are asking. If you call on a student before you ask the question, most of the rest of the class will disengage. (The only time we would suggest calling on a student first is when you are subtly trying to bring him back to class, a non-disruptive form of behavior management.) Do not let the student off the hook with something like "I don't know," but continue probing, perhaps reducing the depth of your question before following up further. A second wait time is very beneficial after a student responds to allow other students time to think and respond before the teacher responds[8]. This encourages discourse in the classroom instead of a didactic exchange between the teacher and individual students.

In our work over the years, we have found that many teachers are far too quick to say something like "That's right" or "No." Don't steal from the students the obligation and opportunity to think for themselves; lead them so that they can determine the soundness of their own reasoning. Indeed, there are instances when you should answer questions directly or comment on students' responses, but your first reaction should be to answer questions with questions and draw the reactions from the students. When students ask you a question, you quickly need to decide whether you are going to answer it directly, let another student answer it, or respond with another question. We encourage directly answering a question when either a student seems excessively frustrated or if it is a procedural question that doesn't directly involve the concept. If it is something that other students should know or are curious about, encourage them to respond to the question. Finally, when the student question is about the concept or problem at hand, it is appropriate to redirect the question back to the student. For instance, when students say, "I don't understand how to solve this," an effective response is to get them talking more about what they do know and what they don't know. You might say something such as, "Explain how you have attempted to solve the problem and where you seem to be getting stuck." This encourages students to think metacognitively about their own learning instead of relying on you to quickly rescue them. By doing so, they will become more independent in their thinking.

Possibly one of the most valuable things that you can do to improve your instruction is to videotape a class that you teach. Then, draw a line down the middle of a sheet of paper, replay the tape, and record all the questions that you led and how you responded to students on the left column. Next, rethink how you could have asked better questions or responded to students in a manner that improved learning and classroom discourse and record these on the right hand side of the paper. If you are stuck regarding what to change, try doing this activity with a peer. A challenge for you: see if you can have a true, meaningful classroom discussion. We define a discussion by at least 60% of the interaction stemming from student voices. Anything less is a modified lecture.

Pace—Keep it Moving

Learning takes time, so we need to provide sufficient opportunities for students to reflect on new ideas. This does not negate the importance of judicially using and managing time. So how do we determine how to best allocate the time to facilitate the greatest growth in our students? Three specific aspects of management help guide how we gauge the pace of instruction: flow, transitions, and time usage. Also, since games have become an important aspect of instruction in many classes, we will address some tips to consider when using games.

Flow. We all have experienced classes, events, or times when everything seems to come together so seamlessly that time flies by without our recognition. These amazing teaching and learning moments are referred to as being in the flow[9]. The opposite can occur as well when time seems to drag on endlessly. So, when students leave your class are they mumbling, "Where did the time go?" or are they saying, "I never thought that class would end"? This may be one indication whether students were in the flow during class. Ideally, both students and teachers would be in the flow on a regular basis.

Several factors encourage flow: goals or objectives are clear, fear of failure and self-consciousness are not evident, there is immediate feedback, and the level of challenge and skill are both high. This last issue involving the relationship of challenge and skill is a critical component that we as teachers can help regulate. Flow or being "in the zone" exists when, relative to the task at hand, students are both highly skilled and highly challenged at the same time. Formative assessments (discussed in Chapters 2 and 4) provide a quick mechanism to check the level of skill that students possess. If their skill level is low and the challenge is too high, then students become frustrated. This is often the result of improperly scaffolding learning. When skill is high but the challenge is low, then boredom ensues. This happens when expectations are set too low, something that is commonly seen in lower level classes when teachers don't think students can achieve very much. To find flow, we need to know our students and what they are capable of for a given concept being studied.

Yes, we understand that your students are all at different ability levels, so how can flow be achieved for all? Try this. The next time that you provide a math problem in algebra or a Punnett square in biology for students to solve, put two problems on the board instead of one. Tell students that it is important that they solve one or the other. Tell them that the second problem is more challenging than the first, but both are related to the content being studied. What will this technique do? The two problems of different skill levels presented at the same time provide a way to challenge struggling students as well as some of the brightest in the class. It allows every student to demonstrate competence, while also allowing some to be challenged even further. If your experience is anything like ours, you will see that many of the students will opt to try the more challenging problem. In the end, it is our responsibility as educators to make sure that we have challenged everyone who walks through our door to the best of our ability.

Transitions. Part of keeping a class moving and focused on learning is to make sure that transitions are quick and appear seamless. Students need to know exactly what to do next, and there should be a sense of immediacy. If papers are to be turned in, there should be an established routine. For instance, a teacher might say, "Pass papers forward (by an established routine, this means pass all papers forward, then to the right until one person has them all, and then that person is responsible for placing them in the appropriate box at the front), get in your groups to practice your team presentation for five minutes, and then return to your seat for presentations to begin. As you work, I will tell you the order in which the groups will present."

As you transition from a lab investigation to a class discussion, students should know where they are to be, what they should have ready, and when the next portion of the lesson will begin. For instance, as groups are beginning to finish data collection, you could provide a cue to students that they have 5 minutes to finish working on their lab before they are to be back in their seats ready to take notes and engage in a discussion. Provide the reminder again with 2 minutes remaining and then again with 1 minute remaining. This provides clear expectations, but it also allows students some time to get to a good stopping point. Timers work well to help you with this. The amount of time required to transition is dependent on the two portions of the lesson being bridged. When there are lots of materials and lots of things involved, then the transitions are typically longer. Regardless, be clear and follow through consistently.

Time Usage. Closely tied to transitions and flow is time usage. With many middle and high schools now scheduling block or 90-minute classes, using time wisely is imperative to maximizing student learning. Sadly, perhaps the most common use of this time is for the teacher to lecture, model the expected solution method, and then provide the last portion of class for guided practice. However, this is neither effective nor efficient in terms of usage of time and often leads to boredom and students disengaged from learning (and, of course, is contrary to the inquiry-based practices we are advocating in this book). As you plan, keep in mind that students (and adults) effectively concentrate for about 15-20 minutes before beginning to zone out—particularly if they are sedentary and are functioning merely as recipients of knowledge.

To deal with this, you should "chunk" the class into segments; the components of inquiry can help to achieve this. For example, a lesson could begin with a quick 10-15 minute Engage that provides some formative data about students' prior knowledge on inheritance (or whatever the topic might be). This could be a KWHL chart, a formative probe, or a brainstorming session based on the essential questions: How do you get your hair color? Do we inherit personalities? Without resolving students' conceptions at this point, have students embark on an investigation of exploring traits and diseases that we inherit and the process responsible for passing along inherited traits. This Explore phase would likely take the remainder of the class period to finish, so it should be broken into specific and targeted pieces. For instance, you could say something like, "For the next twenty minutes, your team is to use the following resources to help discover how we inherit things. Record your findings individually." You could follow this up with more exploration, assigning more tasks to complete. For example, you could say, "Your team will have to use visuals and share with the class how you believe inheritance occurs." Alternatively, you could bring the class back to compile what they found in an effort to synthesize their results before being challenged with another task.

On days when you need to reinforce a major concept (which should be often), the lesson can be broken down into small rapidly moving chunks that all support the same concept. For example, you could have students work a problem in a small team (5 minutes), discuss solutions and their process including various solution methods (10 minutes), solve a slightly easier yet related problem individually (5 minutes), discuss challenges and questions (8 minutes), solve a new extension or twist in groups (5 minutes), discuss their solutions (5 minutes), clarify and summarize (5 minutes), take a two-question quiz that emphasizes the process and the key concept (12 minutes). This is an example of a lesson that transitions often while trying to make sure that no one is ever frustrated for more than 5 minutes at a time. It also provides opportunities for you to work with teams and individuals throughout the class. Notice that the class time is not spent just showing a solution. Instead it is about process—how did you solve it, where did you struggle, what are some alternate solutions?

Finally, while many are advocating for longer school days, we suggest that we first improve the use of time during the school day in the current system. Adding more days will only encourage more fluff time until we learn how to maximize the time already allocated to us. Even though the length of the school day or year is likely outside of our control, if we would combine all of the wasted time seen in classes (slow start to class, using instructional time to conduct non-instructional duties such as handing back papers and taking roll, long and ineffective transitions, and behavioral disruptions), then in many cases we could regain weeks of class time that could be focused on student learning. We challenge you to determine how much time you think is wasted in your class, or in your school, or in your district. This is an area where all of us can improve. However, a caution is in order here: be sure not to turn your classroom into a whirlwind of activity. Students need time to think and process what they are learning; make sure you give them sufficient time and opportunities to do so. Just be intentional about how you organize the time.

Games. The use of games to review or practice can be a great motivator. From a management standpoint, two questions should be paramount to your decision to use a particular game: 1) does the time spent learning and reviewing content far exceed the time spent on non-learning activities such as rules and scoring, and 2) are both content and process emphasized in the game? If the answer to either of these is "no," then you might reconsider whether to use the game at all. One of the most common games played in the classroom is *Jeopardy*. While we are fans of the game, in many cases too much time is spent arguing over rules, points, whose turn it is, and what topic and point value should be selected next. None of those things has anything to do with learning. In other more efficient scenarios, we often see the focus on memorization rather than deeper understanding. So find a game you like, and then modify it as appropriate until you are satisfied that it serves the purpose of being highly engaging and focuses heavily on learning.

We have three tips about keeping students engaged. First, find a way to make most of the points come toward the end of the game. This keeps students hooked because they still have a chance up until the end. Second, not all students enjoy competition, so make the game one where everyone can have success. For instance, if your team scores more than "X" number of points, everyone in the group will receive 2 points toward your test grade. Even better, have a question or two at the end that are answered individually. Points for these can be added with the team score to give an overall individual score. Finally, to maximize class time, do not take time to record individual results during class. Collect the papers, score them (this will provide an excellent indicator of how well students individually know the major ideas), and hand them back with their total score the next day.

Immaturity of Students

Teachers commonly lament that their students are just too immature for inquiry. In some settings, students deemed at-risk are also denied inquiry-based approaches because of teachers' fear that behavioral problems may arise. It is true that some students are more adept at working in groups than others and some are better critical thinkers than others, but this should not change your responsibility as a teacher to provide the richest learning experience possible for all students. There are many stories of how the lives of *all* students can be transformed when they are engaged in learning. In particular, students deemed too immature or at-risk are often the ones who benefit the most from inquiry-based instruction. In Chapter 7, you will read about how inquiry changed the future of many at-risk students in a traditional school setting. In other settings, the change can be even more dramatic. One story includes prior work with at-risk students in a dropout recovery program who were considered disruptive and too immature for "normal" classroom instruction. Instead of learning physics and communication skills in a traditional way, we drew on their interests and experience with automobiles, electronics, and welding to create a solar powered vehicle that was raced in a national competition. Students that needed communications credit worked on a team that designed, practiced, and then gave presentations to executives at major corporations to raise money for the project. The third year of the project resulted in winning two national competitions (a 62-mile track race and a three-day trans-state race) and then participation in a competition against other schools, engineers, and corporations in an international solar vehicle race in Japan[10]. There is nothing more exciting as a teacher than to see students succeeding in amazing ways, including being honored by the governor, after being told for ten years or more that they were failures.

Your story doesn't have to be on the same scale to be just as meaningful. The point is that all students are entitled to great instruction—even if that means a little extra work or scaffolding on our part as teachers. Find out their interests and build inquiry-based experiences that focus on these interests. Have them determine questions that they wish to investigate. It really isn't so much that the students are immature or at risk, but rather that they do not see a purpose or have an interest in what they are doing. Connecting science and mathematics to their world can make a huge impact. Certainly an investigation about sports will not interest all students, but it will reach some, and the next investigation can target a different interest. Better still; provide investigations that allow them to personalize their learning to their interest areas. Students will engage when their curiosity and interest have been piqued; their energy will be directed in a positive direction rather than in a manner that disrupts learning for everyone.

Language Skills

When language and communication skills are low, inquiry can provide a great means to engage the learner and begin to bridge some of the deficits at the same time. Those with poor language skills can be either native or non-native English speakers, but the challenge is almost identical. For some reason, the skills are not present to be able to read, write, or communicate on grade level. English Language Learners (ELL) or English as a Second Language (ESL) students that speak little or no English often have the greatest challenge in our classes. We have options as to how we respond. We can seek to engage them as meaningfully as possible, or we can choose to ignore them and just help them slide through the system on the path of least resistance. The former option means that we need to get them in groups hearing, seeing, and interacting to the best of their ability. On your end as a teacher, it means providing diagrams, visuals, and abbreviated notes to assist them as they make sense out of the world. Remember that even though they may be fluent in their own language, you are expecting them to learn a new language and grow their vocabulary at the same time that they are learning important new content.

Labs in science or problem-solving sessions in math that involve concrete manipulatives can be extremely helpful for these students because they can visually observe the world or phenomenon without needing language. However, the degree to which they make sense of the experience will depend on the support that you can provide, their knowledge in the subject area to begin with, and any assistance that can be provided by peers. Though there is debate about whether or not you should try to communicate with ESL students in their native language, there seems to be a general consensus that working with ESL students in English helps them make the transition more quickly. This being said, it seems that greeting the student or exchanging a few pleasantries in their native tongue is a good way to build rapport and show that you care. Even more importantly, having these students work in inquiry-based settings with other students will give them far more opportunities to interact with the content than they will get from listening to a lecture. Your instruction will be differentiated in a manner that will target their needs and make it much more likely that they will learn.

Honors Students

We have found that leading inquiry with honors students can be both enjoyable and rewarding but also very challenging as well. When they see the true value in the inquiry experience, they reap the benefits and see the reward. However, what many forget is that honors students have mastered the game of school and have been extremely successful. By introducing inquiry to these students, you are seen as a danger to their success because you are changing the rules to the game midstream in their education. Now you are requiring them to think, analyze, and question, which may lead to some resistance and frustration.

In most cases, you can work through these fears with them to show them that inquiry promotes critical thinking, something that is essential for success in college and their future careers. Further, inquiry promotes and models life-long learning where we desire to learn more about something and then begin a quest to grow in that area. Finally, you can create increased buy-in from individuals in this group if you can assure them that with some work on their end, you will help to guide them toward success in inquiry. Inquiry-based teaching may be the first time that some of these honors students have been challenged to think. Many have mastered memorizing algorithms and following procedures, so the challenge can also re-engage many who are academically gifted but bored with the current system. Nevertheless, you should expect initial reluctance on their part, and you will often hear them say something like, "Just tell me what to do."

Perhaps the most important thing you can do in this area is to make sure that your summative assessments, those that count for grades, are fully aligned with your instruction. If you teach for understanding but test only algorithms and facts they have memorized, your students will quickly learn that the inquiry-based processes are not important. However, if your assessments expect students to create, apply, analyze, and engage in high-order processes, they will quickly learn that the inquiry-based processes are critical to their success, and these students value success. They will likely still resist initially—after all, you are challenging them in new ways—but they will also understand that what you are asking them to do is essential for their success.

Apathy

Low motivation and apathy are complex issues without a single solution. In prior work, we have argued that apathy rears its head via a combination of eight different archetypes[2]. The expressed apathy is usually the result of prior experiences and situations. For instance, apathy may be a result of anger; it may be due to seeing and feeling failure for years; it may be due to boredom and not being challenged. Regardless, apathy exists in various forms in every classroom. The goal is to confront it and find positive ways to move forward. Just raising your expectations will be enough to reenlist the interest of some.

For the social beings who inhabit your class and seem to be in school solely to meet with their friends, inquiry instruction provides a great compromise. Allowing some conversation with peers, maybe even allowing them at times to have some input as to the people with whom they will work, may help, but you should always carry the expectation that the majority of the conversation centers on the learning. For the downtrodden student, who has experienced years of failure, it is important to create genuine successes early in the year. Challenges can and should be increased as the number of successful experiences grows, but make success attainable. For students with anger issues, realize that the anger is rarely about you. Try to identify the source of the anger and work with the appropriate individuals in order to defuse it so that learning is not hindered. For instance, if there are questions of physical abuse at home, it does no good to send daily emails home expressing to parents that Johnny is not doing his work again today. Instead, after consulting the counselors and other appropriate personnel, realize that this may be a case where it is important to express a concern for the student but also let him know that second to his safety the most important thing is his learning, at least during science or math class. Certainly you have to use good judgment, but keep in mind that a well-run, functioning class is often one of the few safe havens some students have.

When students are struggling for one reason or another, it is easy to want to show compassion by lowering your expectations. However, lowering expectations both enables and encourages academic failure. High, reasonable expectations serve many useful purposes; here they are a way of showing students that you have respect for their abilities and possess optimism for their future. Irrespective of the form that apathy assumes, building personal meaningful relationships with your students helps to reduce apathy and to increase motivation. If students know that you truly care about them, they will be more inclined to participate fully in class. At first, this may be to avoid disappointing you; this is a wonderful, positive beginning. During the year, then work to help them make their motivation more intrinsic so that in the future they will not want to disappoint themselves.

GENERAL ELEMENTS OF WELL-MANAGED CLASSROOMS

Routines

The need for routines and habits is critical for a smoothly operating class that maximizes time. Everything need not be a routine, but when possible routines help reduce unnecessary anxiety in students. Below, we discuss several different types of routines that influence the operation of your class.

General Management. Do your students know when you are ready to begin class or when it is time to move on without you needing to say a word? Is there a bell, a place you stand, a timer that counts down, or a light flash that lets students know when you are ready to begin? The cue may be verbal as well, such as a "Good morning," but the point is you need a consistent behavior to let students know that you are ready to begin. If your class begins with a warm-up activity, students should know that they are to come in, see the warm-up on the board, and be working by the time that the final bell sounds. It is often worth the time to have everyone get up and leave the class and then reenter until they follow the expected routine, which may be to work individually without visiting with friends for the first five minutes of class while you attend to administrative items such as attendance. This also allows you time to check in quickly with students and observe where they are struggling in their problem solving or with the concept being studied. Though routines are especially beneficial when working with students with many forms of special needs, it is good for all students to know such things as how to come in to class, what to do with assignments, what to do as they finish lab investigations, how to work safely in a lab setting, or how to work effectively in teams.

"Dead time" can often lead to disruptions. Because students work at different speeds, they will finish assignments at different times. You can address this in different ways. Many problems or investigations can be solved at multiple levels. You can set a minimum level that all students need to achieve, and then provide additional challenging levels for those who finish early, an excellent way to differentiate instruction. We also like to have a set of challenge problems that we rotate every couple of weeks. You can set a minimum number that all students must complete during a grading period, and expect students to work on these when they have completed their regular assignments (or tests or quizzes); the key is to make sure that students have something meaningful to do.

These challenge problems can have another positive effect: a few years ago we were working with a girl who was failing mathematics and waiting to drop out of school. One supplemental problem caught her attention and she worked on it for more than three weeks by herself (we confess, she was not doing what she was supposed to be doing, but we were thrilled that she was engaged). Though we provided her with some prompting questions, we would not solve it for her. One day, she finally had a breakthrough and completed the solution (it was the type of problem that you know when you've got it). The excitement and joy in her face are still with us today. We can't claim that this one problem caused the turn-around, but the girl did find a new lease on school, ended up passing the class and graduating.

Seating and Space Issues

Should you assign seats or allow students to select them? Regardless of what you decide, you will save considerable time if you have a seating chart, which, of course, can be changed as needed. This speeds up taking role, helps if a substitute is present, and gives everyone a clear place to belong when you need to regroup. Including students' pictures on the chart can be of immense help, both to you at the beginning of the year and to a substitute, though we recognize that many teachers will not have the technology readily available to do this.

As mentioned earlier, we generally recommend assigning groups yourself (though there may be occasions when you allow students some input). It is true that by allowing students to select their own groups, you give them some autonomy, but there will often be students who are left out and lose confidence in themselves. This is especially true in middle school. If you are doing the grouping yourself, we suggest that you have the groups set ahead of class. That way there is no need to spend class time drawing cards for groups or drawing names out of a hat. Regardless of whether you select the groups or students select the groups, the routines should be clear and predictable so that learning time is maximized.

You may also wish to mix up your groups so that student are heterogeneously grouped by ability sometimes and homogeneously grouped at others. By having groups of four that are heterogeneously grouped, it is usually possible to create quick homogeneous pairs from these cooperative groupings of four on occasion. Either way, be intentional about your decision, because there are benefits and challenges with each decision. All things being equal, we recommend heterogeneous groupings—for one, they are closer in representation to the real world. Also be aware of gender as you group students and pay attention to how students interact with one another. Some teachers prefer changing groups every two weeks or so, while others prefer to wait much longer. There's no right or wrong answer here, though our recommendation is to switch things around at least once during a grading period. Groups that go on too long often establish patterns of behavior that can put too much reliance on a single person or let others off the hook.

If you decide to assign groups of four, you can have the group divide into pairs as well for quick activities, though be aware that almost always, due to enrollment or absences, you will have groups of different sizes at any one time. Consequently, a group of 4 that has become 3 cannot be broken up unless you want a student to work alone. If you have a class of, say 29 students, then you might have ten groups, nine with 3 students and one with two students. Alternatively, you could have nine groups, seven with 3 students and two with 4 students. (This can be an interesting inquiry problem for middle school math students!) If you do plan on having students pair up from time to time, it is most efficient that these pairs are next to each other in the seating chart to allow quick conversations without much disturbance and seat moving.

The room size and shape often limit seating configurations, but for cooperative learning environment, students need to be clustered together in teams when possible. Students also need to be able to see a main presentation area that allows them (and you) to show work, examples, and demonstrations to the entire class. The arrangement of lab space is typically somewhat restricted, but traffic flow and safety issues are important. For instance, can the teacher move freely among the seating and the lab stations? Is the distance that students travel to the supply station minimal?

Rules

As adults, we work under a set of assumed rules and guidelines, but as students are growing and developing, establishing and communicating a common set of principles to guide interactions is important. We recommend having rules, but the list should be short—we suggest five or fewer. It can be very beneficial to allow students to participate in formulating the rules for the class. This democratic process will likely end up in about the same place as you originally intended if facilitated well, but it has the advantage of giving students a voice in the classroom. Remember a rule is only beneficial if you are willing to enforce it, and you must enforce rules consistently. There is something about human nature that desires to push boundaries from time to time, but one sure recipe for disaster is to be inconsistent in applying rules. To go weeks ignoring a rule and then suddenly begin enforcing it will make students angry and rebellious.

There is not a golden set of rules, but one nice global set of rules would be[11]:

1. Act in a safe and healthy way.
2. Treat all property with respect.
3. Respect the rights and needs of others.
4. Take responsibility for learning.

Safety. Regardless of the rules and expectations held, there is one non-negotiable—learning must be done safely. Accidents can and will happen in a classroom, but making sure that students are engaged in learning in a safe manner is critical. This is especially true in science class, though it can be a concern in mathematics classes as well. Safety begins by using materials and equipment as they were intended to be used, storing and handling chemicals properly, making sure to review safety with students before they begin, and cleaning up properly after finishing. In an inquiry setting where it is possible for students to engage in related though different investigations simultaneously, it is important that all procedures are approved and initialed before groups begin their exploration. There should be clear consequences when teams vary from a procedure without approval. This ensures that you are aware of what students are doing, while also allowing them some needed freedom to explore in unique ways.

The security of equipment is closely related to the safety issues. Unfortunately, not everyone believes that stealing is a bad thing, so it is important to have efficient and quick means to make sure all equipment is accounted for before class is dismissed. Once something leaves the class, it is nearly impossible to recover it. For calculators, having a box with the exact number of slots or a hanging holder with pouches allows you to scan quickly to see if all have been returned before dismissing. Electronic balances are particularly popular, so either find a way to lock them down or make sure that all are accounted for at the end of each class. In classes where students will frequently be needing access to items such as glassware, a check-out and check-in policy can be effective. This policy requires that students check out and sign off that they have specific items, which can be locked in a drawer at the end of the period. Then, at the end of the term or year, they show that they still have all the items and check them back in. This could be done with glassware, computers, calculators, or anything that students need to succeed.

Technology

Technology has much to offer when used properly. By far, the most frequent use of technology has to be the ubiquitous PowerPoint presentations. When PowerPoint first began to be used in classrooms, it was captivating because it was flashy and novel. What has continued to occur is that the novelty has worn off but the flash often overshadows a true demonstration of content. For student presentations, make sure that the rubrics are about clarity, knowledge, and depth of thought, not about nice graphics or pretty pages. PowerPoint also allows teachers to blister through massive amounts of material without clear understanding being achieved. We suggest that PowerPoint notes, in general, not exceed 15 minutes of class. Realize that students tune out after 15-20 minutes (less for elementary students), but you are still holding them responsible for the material. Consequently, notes should be interspersed with opportunities for students to engage in the material. For instance, after five minutes of notes (2-3 screens) have students turn to their neighbor and discuss the key points and determine what they are still confused about. This allows notes to be more interactive, and it provides you with quick feedback as to where students are still struggling.

There are many other technologies that allow students to interact with key concepts, including scientific and graphing calculators, spreadsheets, probes (e.g., motion detectors, light detectors), and many software packages. One of the great advantages to these is that large amounts of data can be gathered and analyzed rapidly. The challenge is to make sure that the technology becomes background and the content being studied becomes foreground. Technology becomes an impediment to learning in the following situations: computers take too long to boot up to justify the time spent using them, the learning curve on the software is not intuitive and takes too long to learn, the hardware and software are unstable and crash often, and students are overly distracted by the wiz-bang-wow of the technology. Remember that when technology is ineffective, it provides another opportunity for behavioral problems and management issues. Let's consider some scenarios that we have seen arise as teachers have tried to employ technology.

Scenario #1: Thirty minutes of class is remaining and you want students to work on an interactive program from eLearning called Gizmos. This sounds great until you analyze the situation more carefully. The computers are slow to boot up, typically taking 5-8 minutes from the time the students get the computers from the laptop cart. Couple this with another few minutes consumed because students forgot passwords and forgot which assignments they need to complete. So what looked like 30 minutes of learning is 7-12 minutes of set up plus 5-7 minutes of clean up, leaving only about 11-18 minutes for learning—a 40-63% waste of time! One solution is to begin class with the computers up and running. Students can be setting up computers before the tardy bell rings. They can begin working on a warm-up activity while the computers are working through the boot-up screens.

Scenario #2: There is a program that you want to use with students that will be used only 2 or 3 times during the school year. The program takes about half a class period before students are able to use it effectively. In this case, you need to determine what the value of this learning is. If you think it is critical for students to use this program or application because it greatly enhances learning, then the time may be well justified. In any case, reflect carefully on the learning objective and then seek out the best manner to achieve the objective. It may be more effective just using paper and pencil, or there may be a program that is much more user friendly and can save time.

Scenario #3: Students tried logging onto the recommended URLs only to find that most had been blocked or that the sites are no longer available. Always check URLs the morning they will be used on a computer that students will be using to access them. If sites are often blocked or if the internet is too slow, then students will quickly become disruptive as they get frustrated. One solution may be to make some hard copies of several of the sites for groups to use. If you have a folder with one copy of each site in it for each group, this will allow them to keep working. This is not the greenest solution, but when platforms and programs are unstable they become a deterrent to learning. Further, if these are sites that you are likely to use in the future, then these folders can be kept in files for later use. Finally, you should copy only the most critical sites that provide the content that students must have to succeed. When the internet is functional, they can go to some of the other sites that may be more interactive or contain video. Another option for those who are a little more tech savvy includes partially downloading webpages to computers. This makes them available when the computers are offline. A final management tip for computer use: position yourself so that you can see the screens of most computers in a quick glance. If students typically all face the front of the class, then you may wish to be in the back.

This tip is also applicable to classroom management in general and to inquiry-based instruction in particular. As you circulate through the room to monitor individuals or groups, position yourself so that you can see the majority of students. Getting down to students' eye level is important for rapport, and positioning yourself properly is important to be able to see what is going on throughout the classroom.

DISCIPLINE PLAN

Despite all of your efforts to be proactive in managing behavior effectively, you will still experience times when you find yourself losing control. The natural human reaction is to become louder, faster, and higher—yet all three tend to feed the misbehavior. Take a deep breath and very consciously look directly at the students, maintaining eye contact with individual students for three or four seconds. Then, lower your voice, slow down, and talk in a lower pitch. When students learn that they cannot rattle you (or at least think that you are not rattled), they will, far more often than not, no longer have the need to find and push you to your limits. When we are calm, students will have a tendency to be calmer. Notice, we said calmer not calm. Not surprisingly, when students are angry, it is difficult to get them to calm down immediately, but when we slow things down, reduce our own anxiety level, allow a little more thinking time, and remain calm on our end, then students have a tendency to mirror what we are modeling.

Even in the most proactive, well-managed class, misbehavior will occur. So what should be done when this happens? First realize that misbehavior stems from four issues: seeking attention, seeking power, seeking revenge, or seeking isolation[12]. Often misbehavior results from a combination of these root causes. For instance, students who refuse to turn in any work and seem intent on failing the course may be seeking power and revenge. The revenge may be to get back at parents who have hurt them emotionally. Students quickly realize that grades are one of the few areas where they actually have almost complete power and control. They can choose to fail or choose to succeed, but no one can ultimately force students to achieve.

Many schools have a discipline plan, but to provide a little support for those who need it, any plan should have a series of steps that advance depending on the severity and the frequency of the behavior. Behavioral interventions fall along the following continuum that spans from low intervention to extensive: extinction, nonverbal desists, verbal desists, reprimands, time-outs, and severe punishment that ultimately could end in expulsion from the school[13].

Be sure to think through your consequences. If you do have cumulative consequences (e.g., for the first violation, you warn the student; for the second violation, the student comes in after class, and so on), make sure you know when things start over. Is each class period a fresh start? Each week? Each quarter? In our experience, we have seen many teachers with lists of rules and consequences who have not thought this through, and their rules ended up causing more problems than they solved. Whatever you decide should be clear and logical to both you and your students.

If the behavior is more of an annoyance and you know the student is seeking attention, then begin with extinction, hoping that ignoring the behavior will help it to cease. Then, find a good time to give positive attention by catching the student in an appropriate moment that can be praised. Your main purpose with extinction is to prevent the student from receiving reinforcement for the annoying behavior, so do not ignore the behavior if the student is getting some type of reinforcement from others or, of course, if the behavior persists.

When behavior surpasses minor annoyances, action is needed. In most cases, the "evil eye" is enough of a nonverbal desist to stop the behavior with minimal to no interruption of instructional time. Being successful with this relates directly to the presence you have established in the class. Sometimes the eye doesn't work, leading to the next levels of intervention, which are often the most troubling to teachers. These infractions involve an ongoing disturbance that, when multiplied by several students, can be effective in stopping the majority of classroom instruction. Though the need for interventions can be minimized greatly with many of the proactive suggestions that have been mentioned earlier in the chapter, you will still, inevitably, have to deal with disruptive behaviors. When the need arises, use interventions that are timely, personal, appropriate, and with the future in mind.

Timely means that the intervention should happen immediately following the infraction or as soon thereafter as possible. Often we have to find the next best time, typically at the end of class, but definitely before the beginning of the next class, or while students are working in teams on an assignment. The goal is to avoid embarrassing students in front of their peers; this almost always backfires in the end. This brings us to the personal aspect. When we know what students really care about, then we can begin to plan appropriate interventions. For instance, if playing on the basketball team is the most important thing to the student, then use this as leverage when needed. This involves a personal conversation first to let the student know what is unacceptable and what the consequences will be if the misbehavior continues—having to miss practice and spend time in detention, visiting with the coach, etc. The last thing that you want to do is totally remove a student from basketball because that is the motivator. Just remember: don't threaten if you are not willing to follow through in the event it occurs again. Also, corrective actions should be directed toward individuals and not entire groups unless the issue is so widespread that you cannot distinguish the individuals involved. (If this happens often, improve the way you monitor the class.) Next, make sure the consequences are appropriate for the behavior. There is no need to suspend a student for two days for not turning in homework for two consecutive days. Lastly, remember to keep the future in mind. Once all the dust has cleared, remember that in 99.9% of the cases you will be working with this student for the remainder of the year, so think about building a win-win. You win when the students comply with your needs. The student wins when he succeeds in your class and has not been embarrassed in the process.

REWARD

We can easily get lost in the punishment side of things and forget the more powerful aspects found when using rewards. Much has been written about the merits of intrinsic and extrinsic motivation[14]. And, while we prefer intrinsic rewards, such as the satisfaction and confidence that are derived from academic success, over extrinsic rewards, there is a very real issue that is often left out of the discussion. Our society and most early schooling is built around an extrinsic reward system (e.g., grades, candy, physical awards), so realize that there are many competing factors that are going against your efforts to use intrinsic rewards. In the end, remember that extrinsic rewards lead to short-term motivation and intrinsic rewards are valuable for encouraging long-term motivation, which, in turn, leads to life-long learning. Regardless of the reward structure used, be careful to award academic credit only for academic learning. Many schools have begun to realize this and have policies, but we still see students getting points on their grade for bringing cans for the canned food drive. The cause is excellent, but it is not an academic activity.

Although this book focuses on improving inquiry-based instruction, we felt it necessary to address the greatest fear of teachers as a whole—effectively managing a classroom. We hope that the major issues that interfere with successfully facilitating inquiry have been addressed here. This is not meant to be a comprehensive guide, but the suggestions provide many proven and beneficial techniques for effective management. Finally, while the issues of successful management are fairly global, you will find many issues that need to be addressed in teams or at the school level. We hope this has provided the impetus necessary to begin those critical conversations.

ENDNOTES

1.   Barmby, P., Improving teacher recruitment and retention: The importance of workload and pupil behaviour. *Educational Research* 2006, 48, (3), 247-265.

2.   Marshall, J. C., *Overcoming Student Apathy: Motivating Students for Academic Success.* Rowman & Littlefield Publishers, Inc.: Lanham, MD, 2008.

3.   Everson, C. M.; Randolph, C. H., Perspectives on classroom management in learning-centered classrooms. In *New directions for teaching practice and research,* Waxman, H.; Walberg, H. J., Eds. McCutchan: Berkeley, CA, 1999; pp 249-268.

4.   Marshall, J., Building knowledge and intrigue. *Science Scope* 2006, 30, (2), 34-39.

5.   Mergendoller, J. R.; Markham, T.; Ravitz, J.; Larmer, J., Pervasive management of project based learning: Teachers as guides and facilitators. In *Handbook of classroom management: Research, practice, and contemporary issues,* Everston, C. M.; Weinstein, C. S., Eds. Lawrence Erlbaum Associates, Inc.: Mahwah, NJ, 2006; pp 583-614.

6.   Lotan, R. A., Managing groupwork in the heterogeneous classroom. In *Handbook of classroom management: Research, practice, and contemporary issues,* Evertson, C. M.; Weinstein, C. S., Eds. Lawrence Erlbaum Associates, Inc.: Mahwah, NJ, 2006.

7.   Rowe, M., Wait time: Slowing down may be a way of speeding up. *American Educator* 1987, 11, (1), 38-43, 47.

8.   Tobin, K., The role of wait time in higher cognitive learning. *Review of Educational Research* 1987, 56, 69-95.

9.   Csikszentmihalyi, M., *Finding flow.* Basic Books: New York, 1997.

10.   Marshall, J., Racing with the sun--Inquiry approach to teaching physics. *The Science Teacher* 2004, 71, (1), 40-43.

11.   Grandmount, R. P., Judicious discipline: A constitutional approach for public high schools. *American Secondary Education* 2003, 31, (3), 97-117.

12.   Dreikers, R.; Pepper, F.; Grunwald, B., *Maintaining sanity in the classroom: Classroom management techniques*. 2nd ed.; Taylor Francis: Florence, KY, 1998.

13.   Cruickshank, D. R.; Jenkins, D. B.; Metcalf, K. K., *The act of teaching*. 4th ed.; McGraw-Hill: New York, 2006.

14.   Kohn, A., *Punished by rewards: The trouble with gold stars, incentive plans, A's, praise, and other bribes*. Houghton Mifflin: Boston, 1993.

CHAPTER 7

DEVELOPING A PLAN FOR SUCCESS

Without motivation, a clear plan, and personal resolve, professional development efforts inevitably fail. We are apt to revert back to the familiar and the comfortable—even if we know that our current path is largely unsuccessful—unless we are convinced that the change is realistic, attainable, and worthwhile. In this chapter, we discuss ways to transform practice to improve the quality of inquiry instruction and learning. Our assumption is that motivation and personal resolve are present and that assistance is now needed to achieve the vision.

DEALING WITH CHANGE

Undoubtedly, change is difficult, and it may seem that inquiry is just the latest fad in a long line of educational innovations. However, this is simply not true. Though the terminology may vary in different domains, the concept of inquiry has been promoted for decades[1,2]. Specifically, inquiry maximizes the learning experience for students. The fundamental question at this point becomes whether or not you believe change is needed. Do all of your students truly know what they should know? Can they investigate ideas and solve problems that they haven't seen before, or do they primarily mimic the procedures or steps you have shown them? Even then, do they remember the major ideas a month or two after the assessment? Can they use mathematics and science to make predictions, estimate outcomes, investigate problems, think critically, or communicate knowledge effectively?

A couple of years ago a highly regarded middle school teacher told us that he simply needed to tell his students what to do, that conceptual understanding would follow when they were older. Though he felt successful in "telling" rather than engaging students in learning, his approach is based on an assumption that students somehow have an epiphany where they suddenly can think deeply and critically. The reality is that if you want your students to learn to think critically, then they need to be provided frequent opportunities to develop their critical thinking skills. Simply having them memorize a list of terms, follow a prepared lab procedure, or mimic an algorithm is not sufficient.

It may be human nature to resist change. However, with commitment and guidance, not just through administrative decree, you can move from desire to implementation. The rewards are well worth the hard work. You have to determine for yourself whether your current practice is achieving sufficient results. If you believe improvement is a necessity, then transitioning to an inquiry-based approach is one change that can make a substantial difference in student performance. This is what we experienced; traditional approaches just were not working, so we sought something different. Our evidence shows that change is indeed possible, and that inquiry instruction promotes greater engagement in the learning process and deeper understanding of the content.

Although we advocate for making several incremental changes, it is also possible to make whole-scale changes. The following true story illustrates the potential of an inquiry-based approach relative to student learning.

Before we had fully developed the 4E x 2, the EQUIP, and the Web Tool (but were nonetheless promoting inquiry-based practice), a teacher in a professional development class of ours became very excited about inquiry. She had known something was missing from her practice, but she didn't know what and didn't know how to fix it. As it turns out, an inquiry-based approach was exactly what she wanted.

Both she and her administration were aware that their current efforts to remediate students who were struggling were not working. Though they could identify which students were at risk early on and they tried to support these students with extra classes, the overwhelming majority still dropped out of school at their first opportunity. Mathematics was identified as the key problem area.

The teacher, Cathy Plowden, invited us to work with her the following year. With the support of her administration, we undertook teaching 15 of the lowest achieving students, all of whom had failed eighth grade math and summer school but were still promoted to ninth grade. We selected a range of contextual problems to ensure that we would address all of the "big ideas," and decided not to use a text. Students worked in groups of three and were regrouped approximately every three weeks.

Over the course of the year, students were assigned 22 problems. (Compare that with the 30 or so "problems" that many teachers assign every night!) All of the problems were named to help trigger students' recall later on and used a context to connect to students' prior experiences and knowledge. Further, all had several prompting questions to help lead the students from the specifics of the context toward the underlying ideas. Students solved all of the problems in groups but were held individually accountable for writing up and presenting their solutions. Most class periods were spent working on the problems, though Cathy did lead whole class discussions a couple of times per week. Approximately twice a week, she also provided some skill practice, but this was done only after the need for the skills arose in the problems. We did not focus on automating skills through lots of repetition; these were students who needed help with fundamental ideas and understandings, all of the way back to whole number addition and subtraction, and we recognized that they had not been successful in the past with classes that emphasized repetition and automation. In summary, we employed an inquiry-based strategy with a problem-based curriculum.

As the year passed, we were excited to discover how well students remembered what they had done throughout the year. They often found connections on their own, saying things like "That's just like the Cricket Problem we did at the beginning of the year." Math finally started making sense to them. Of the 15 students, one moved away, and one dropped out due to family issues, but of the 13 who remained, all passed the class; all passed the state's "Exit Exam" on their first attempt; and all graduated from high school on schedule. These results show that students who have struggled in school can benefit from inquiry-based practices and achieve when the expectations are consistent, attainable, and high.

Granted we had some definite advantages, specifically a team approach so there were usually two educators in the class, administrative support, and no disciplinary issues. Nonetheless, these students experienced success, most for the first time. Cathy is convinced that the biggest cause for the students' success was the inquiry-based approach. Perhaps even more importantly, since this first effort with inquiry-based instruction, Cathy has had similar, extremely positive results with Algebra I, Algebra II, Probability and Statistics, and Geometry. She also takes an inquiry-based approach to a remedial class for students in her school who have failed the examination the State requires for high school graduation, with exceptional results.

We recognize that the conditions in Cathy's initial experience with inquiry-based instruction are unlikely to be duplicated elsewhere, and, as stated earlier, we recommend incremental changes for most teachers, not a complete, abrupt shift in instructional practice. No matter the speed of the change, we are convinced that effective inquiry instruction can have a positive, significant impact upon the lives of students as it is adopted throughout classrooms, schools, and districts.

INCREMENTAL CHANGES TO INDIVIDUAL PRACTICE

Most teachers are not able to change everything in the instructional structure within one year as Cathy did, but an intentional, incremental approach can also be powerful and allow teachers to acclimate to the changes before implementing more. As discussed at the conclusion of Chapter 4, EQUIP gives an excellent vehicle for making incremental changes.

After an observation, preferably by a peer or by someone else whom you trust, study the ratings for each indicator. As we suggested in Chapter 4, if you are primarily a Level 1 teacher, join

NCTM or NSTA if you have not already done so, and begin regular reading of articles in *The Mathematics Teacher, The Science Teacher*, or other professional journals. Learn what others are doing and how they're going about it. Think about your practice, and craft a vision of the ideal teacher, someone you want to be.

Then pick one of the indicators (certainly no more than two or three) that you want to improve. Study the rubrics associated with the higher ratings and discuss them with someone, perhaps the person who conducted the initial observation. Determine what it would take to achieve the next higher rating and work toward this on your lessons for at least the next week, of course only on those lessons in which you believe inquiry-based instruction is the best strategy.

Once you are satisfied, pick an indicator from one of the other factors (remember that we have focused on four: Instruction, Discourse, Assessment, and Curriculum) and work on it until you achieve consistent improvement. Continue in this manner until you have improved on four indicators, one on each factor. After you are satisfied with your progress on these four indicators, we suggest that you not tackle another indicator until these four are virtually automatic in your own practice. Continue to reassess your practice to ensure that you have not regressed on any of the other indicators or reverted back to your old practice on any of the reformed indicators. Perhaps several weeks, even several months, will pass until you are ready to tackle the next cycle of improvement.

By taking the indicators one at a time and by giving yourself many opportunities to improve in single areas, you will find that the change will not be overwhelming. Just as our children and our students often grow in small steps so that we do not see them changing, so too can your practice grow smoothly and gradually. Over a period of many months or even a year or two, however, the overall change is dramatic. Make sure you have a clear vision of the ideal teacher, and continue to strive for that as your target. Even though no one ever becomes the ideal teacher, we know that we can always improve.

WORKING TOGETHER TO CHANGE PRACTICE

Change, as we have said, can be difficult. Though teachers are individuals and must be the instruments of their own change, transforming practice is much easier when group support is available to share ideas, to provide encouragement, to help set goals and assess progress, and to lend emotional support for the inevitable difficulties that will be encountered.

The Importance of Cohorts

When we first started working with teachers on the 4E x 2 Model and the other ideas promoted in this book, we worked with teachers from schools throughout the district and not teachers from individually targeted schools. Each participant had at most one other teacher from her home school working with us. This resulted in unnecessary challenges. Though we tried to follow up regularly with each of the teachers, traveling to many different schools consumed more of our time than actually working with the teachers. Even more importantly, the teachers did not have a support network to help them overcome immediate challenges. Though we met as a group several times during the academic year, the teachers needed more.

We learned that for a major shift, such as one to a more inquiry-based practice, we have greater success when we target an entire math or science department at a school. To do so, we first have district leaders identify a specific school or two to target. If the building level principal is supportive of the effort, then we set up a meeting with all of the math and science teachers in the school. During this meeting, we present the specifics about the program, spelling out what they are committing to do and what we are committing to do. We emphasize the importance of them being vested in the program, so we request that they meet among themselves to decide whether or not they want to work with us. Our threshold for taking on a cohort is 60%; if fewer than 60% of the department either does not want to or cannot work with us during the summer and the following year, then we will not target that school, believing that the school is not at a place to make a commitment toward change. This past year we had to postpone the involvement of a potential partner school until they are able to meet or exceed the 60% participation level. Our experience has confirmed that having this strong building commitment, which establishes a cohort group within the school, makes a huge difference in what teachers are able to accomplish.

Though we hope that teachers who are not part of a department-wide or school-wide effort will adopt an inquiry-based approach, we know that they may feel that they are swimming upstream without any ladders or supports to help them along the way. It takes special teachers, such as Cathy, with a deep commitment to make this transformation alone. Nevertheless, it is possible. By reading, joining professional organizations such as NCTM and NSTA, attending conferences, and seeking outside help, they too can change their practice. Though they may not have an ally in the room next door, they can build their own support networks.

Sustaining the Momentum

One of the primary means for sustaining change is to be part of a group that is embracing the same change. Making significant changes is extremely difficult when you are alone; it can be extremely beneficial to be part of a group that is facing the same challenges and can support each other along the way. Being part of a group can make a tremendous difference for most teachers who wish to change their practice. Building cohorts helps to encourage change, but how is change sustained? Teams, departments, or schools can help keep the momentum going by encouraging continued conversations that focus on, among other things, critiquing practice, setting goals, brainstorming solutions to new challenges, assessing student work samples collaboratively, and measuring progress. Our hope is that by describing our professional development efforts, we may help trigger some ideas that will work for you.

Our professional development programs run for two years. In the first year, we work with at least 60% of the math and science departments from our targeted schools. We spend two intensive weeks in the summer and have four group follow-up sessions during the academic year. We also visit teachers regularly in their classrooms during the academic year, spending, on average, one full class period with each teacher at least once a month. During these visits, we may observe and provide feedback or, depending on the teacher's wishes, co-teach, fill in for the teacher so that she may observe someone else, or support the teacher in any other way requested of us. Obviously this is very time intensive, and not all providers of professional development can invest so much in a school. Nevertheless, we believe teachers need on-going support over a significant length of time, an idea supported by research[3-5].

Each year we begin to work with a new school, so we are unable to have such a strong presence in a partner school during the second year. However, we want to ensure that the teachers with whom we have worked maintain whatever momentum they have established during the first year and continue on the path to sustainable change. To accomplish this, we rely on the teachers themselves.

For the second year, we invite some teachers from the previous year to join us in an Advanced Professional Development Leadership Institute. The teachers who participate must have expressed an interest, demonstrated a commitment to inquiry, achieved or nearly achieved an overall rating of proficiency on EQUIP, have the respect of the other teachers, and have the support of their building principal. Our target is to get between one-third and one-half of the teachers with whom we worked to become involved in the Advanced Institute.

For a full week in the summer, we work with these teachers on the following goals:

- Reinforce the planning and implementation of inquiry-based instruction,
- Develop proficiency on the use of EQUIP, and
- Create a school-wide plan for the following academic year.

The school-wide plan is the cornerstone of our efforts. It must include monthly meetings in which these teacher leaders will meet with their departments to share ideas and support the other teachers who worked with us the previous year. The plan must also include a strategy for working with new teachers in the school in a manner that will be supportive but not coercive.

After this first week, the teachers in the Advanced Institute then help us as we work with a new school during the two-week, initial Professional Development Institute. Each teacher leader joins a team of two or three teachers and guides them as these new teachers experience inquiry and then work on developing an exemplar lesson that targets one of the big ideas they will teach in the fall. They also try to ensure that the teachers in their group have the necessary depth of content knowledge.

Toward the conclusion of the third week, our Advanced Institute teachers refine their school-wide plans with their fresh insights gleaned from working with the new teachers. In addition to determining how they might best sustain a transformation toward inquiry-based practices back in their home schools, they also, of course, have new exemplar lessons that they can share, just as they can share the exemplar lessons that they created the previous year with the new teachers.

With this strategy, we can add, depending on the size, one or two new schools to our efforts each year. More importantly, we are setting in place a means for sustaining growth, a means that allows the schools to stand on their own. We remain available to serve as resources, but just as your goals should be to help your students become independent learners, one of our goals is to help our schools sustain inquiry-based practices on their own.

Dealing with Faculty and Administrative Turnover

Turnover in schools is inevitable. Though teachers are less likely to leave the teaching profession when they gain confidence and competence, family situations change, retirements occur, and different opportunities arise. Another purpose of our Advanced Leadership Institute is to smooth transitions by having multiple teachers from each department committed to sustaining the change. If one member leaves the school, there are still others available to keep the momentum going.

By having school leaders who are committed to inquiry-based instruction, teachers new to the school will have the support they need if they want to be part of the process. And, with a department that is moving together, new personnel are far more likely to want to adopt inquiry-based practices.

When the administration changes, different issues may arise, particularly if a new administrator is averse to inquiry-based instruction. By having school-wide teacher leaders who are well respected, effective in their practice, active in professional organizations, and knowledgeable about some of the research that supports their efforts, conversations may be possible that will convince the new administrator to take a "wait and see" approach before nixing the changes that are taking place.

As with many things, the key is to anticipate and to plan. Expect a change in both teachers and administration. Become a leader in your school and know what you want, why you want it, and why you believe it will work. You may still come across those who will block your path, but your chances are much better for success if you think ahead. Perhaps most importantly of all, believe in your approach but be inclusive of others who are on the fence or new to the school. They may just end up being your strongest supporters.

WORKING THROUGH CHALLENGES TO ACHIEVING SUCCESS

Inevitably, you will face many challenges, some great and some small, as you try to transform your instruction to one that is inquiry-based and develops concepts at deep levels. In this final section, we address several of the challenges that we have experienced ourselves and seen with the teachers, schools, and districts with whom we have worked.

Conflicting Beliefs

Beliefs About Mathematics, Science, and Teaching. One of the challenges that we have encountered involves a difference in beliefs about what mathematics is, what science is, and what teaching is. Different beliefs can lead to differences in practice. Is mathematics a bag of tricks that can be accessed depending on the type of situation a person is facing? Is it a set of universal truths to be discovered (a Platonic approach), or is it a human creation (a problem-solving approach)? Is it an art or a science? In our view, there is room for all of the above beliefs. Consequently, we believe that different teaching strategies are appropriate at different times. However, we also believe that conceptual development and proficiency in the process skills (problem solving, reasoning, communication, connections, and representation) are at the forefront of what is important, and to achieve success in these areas, inquiry-based strategies are often the best. Inquiry-based instruction develops habits of mind in approaching problems, reasoning through them, communicating this reasoning, connecting ideas to other ideas in mathematics or science and to the real world, and representing these ideas in multiple ways. And when done effectively, these processes lead toward deep understanding of math and science content.

In science, there is less debate about what the discipline is, but too often we see teachers tell about science, rather than actually teach science. Science is not simply a list of facts to be memorized; instead it involves understanding the scientific process and the nature of science, where results are tentative but based on the best understanding that we currently have. We challenge you to define your discipline and then to align your practice with this definition; do not merely tell students things that scientists have learned, but instead help them to engage in the process of exploring science.

What, in fact, is teaching, and what do you believe about it? Because most of us have been steeped in lectures, we tend to view teaching as telling. Thus many assume that our job as teachers is to tell students what we know about our discipline. Though there are certainly times when this is appropriate, we believe there should be far more times when we guide students, helping them develop ideas that they can use and apply in new situations.

This requires that teachers are masters of their content who impart learning through a guided venture. The truth is that teaching with inquiry-based strategies, not just providing activities, requires deeper content and pedagogical knowledge than teaching in a more traditional manner. To be clear, we do not expect students to discover for themselves what it has taken human beings thousands of years to learn. We are not espousing free discovery and expecting students to generate all of their ideas on their own. But we can and should guide, lead, prod, question, challenge, and encourage our students, helping them build upon their own prior knowledge and experiences so that they learn at deeper levels. Teaching effectiveness is a continuum where we should always strive to improve, so we hope that you reflect upon your beliefs, develop your vision of what effective teaching is, and constantly move in that direction.

Problematizing Practice. If a teacher does not see a need to change, then change will surely not happen. This is often referred to as a need to problematize practice, and there is a significant amount of research to justify this claim[6-8]. How do your students respond when confronted with real-world problems? Do they tend to avoid them? Do they remember and are they able to apply what you taught a month ago? Do topics that have previously been taught still look foreign to your students? Teachers at all levels complain to some degree about issues surrounding these questions, but you should determine which ones are serious issues for you, your department, and your school. Finally, if your students are not living up to high, but reasonable expectations, then we look closely at what needs to be changed in your teaching practice.

Inquiry-based instruction can make a huge impact in this area. If you and those with whom you work do believe that there is more to teaching and learning, then you have seen a need for change. This is the first crucial step to transforming practice: recognizing that there is a problem.

Discrepancy between Beliefs and Practice. Years ago, Alba Thompson[9] and Tom Cooney[10] wrote convincingly about how teachers often believe one thing but practice another. Many teachers who believe in an inquiry-based approach may not have the confidence, the knowledge, the tools, or the support to implement it regularly and/or effectively in the classroom. Our point here is to encourage you to be reflective about your practice. Do you teach in ways that you believe are most effective? If you believe in inquiry-based instruction but do not employ it regularly, try to identify the reasons for this discrepancy. Then, seek help from peers, professional conferences, providers of professional development experiences, and journals that will fill in the gaps for you.

Depth of Content Knowledge

Some may think that teachers using an inquiry-based approach do very little teaching. In fact, Cathy Plowden has often said that, until they really understood what she was doing, her administrators used to tell her that they never caught her teaching. The truth is that inquiry-based teaching requires more on the teacher's part, particularly in the area of content knowledge, advanced preparation, and understanding of how students think. It is far simpler to teach in the traditional manner when you know you won't be challenged and students won't be seeking connections or clarifications that you have not thought of yourself. This is certainly one of the scarier aspects of inquiry-based teaching, especially for younger teachers who have not yet established their credibility with their students or administrators.

Inquiry-based teaching does indeed require greater content knowledge. However, keep in mind that no one knows more than a small fraction of any domain. Our main point is that if you yourself are always looking for connections and are trying to understand why things work the way they do, you will be serving your students as an excellent role model as well as engaging them in meaningful learning. Be willing to say things such as, "I don't know, but let's see what we can discover." And then be sure to follow through. Attend professional conferences; we never fail to learn something useful at NCTM, NSTA, and other conferences. Talk with other teachers, and be willing to ask questions.

One of the things we tell our teachers is that when students ask a content-related question, they are paying you a compliment. They care about what you are teaching and they want to gain knowledge. Though there are times when you should answer questions directly to avoid generating too much anxiety and frustration, most often it's perfectly okay to answer their question with other questions, perhaps even to the point where you'll get the ultimate compliment when they say something like, "Never, mind, we can figure this out for ourselves." You want to develop critical thinkers and life-long learners, so praise questions and get excited about them. When students, not you, are prompting the "Engage" stage of inquiry-based instruction, you have made great strides. One of the worst things a teacher can do is to stifle students' questions and curiosity. Yes, it may take you away from your excellent lesson plan, and, yes, it may take more time, but think about the benefits. Even if you have to defer the question to a later time, do not ignore it.

Using Non-Inquiry Materials in an Inquiry-Based Way
Most texts do not take an inquiry-based approach to achieve conceptual development. In fact, they tend to do the reverse, beginning with a formal, generalized concept, providing definitions of terms, and then showing examples of how to apply the ideas or algorithms. In other words, despite some strong evidence that we learn best through experience and by inductive thinking, most texts take a deductive approach, working from the general to the specific. Although we encourage teachers to think of texts as resources rather than the curriculum, we are realistic enough to know that many teachers, especially those in their first couple of years of teaching or those who are teaching a course for the first or second time, rely on their texts to guide their instruction. So how can they use an inquiry-based strategy when their texts do not?

Our recommendation is to work backwards within the text, of course, using good judgment in your planning and implementation. Most traditional math texts have some word problems toward the back of each section. Find one or two of these problems that you think students can grasp. You may need to modify them so that students can understand and relate to their context; inquiry-based instruction is not effective if students cannot connect a problem in some way to their own experiences and understanding. The goal here is not to challenge the students with a real "stumper," but to present them with something upon which they can build understanding. At times, you may need to create or find a totally different problem or take one from a different section, but more often than not, you will be able to find one in the current section.

Use these problems to develop concepts, showing the need for the ideas and how and why they work. In other words, build *toward* the concepts rather than *from* them. The concepts, and definitions at times, are the culmination of the lesson. Consider, for example, how absolute value is introduced in many math texts. It is defined formally, something such as $|a| = a$ if $a > 0$ or if $a = 0$; $|a| = -a$ if $a < 0$. While correct, this definition does virtually nothing to develop conceptual understanding of absolute value.

Instead, consider the "Where Should It Be?" problem introduced in Chapter 4 in this book. In this problem, a fast food chain sets up five restaurants along a highway located mile markers 2, 4, 16, 28, and 50. There are five trucks, one to go to each of the five restaurants (a single truck cannot service more than one restaurant on a trip.) The problem is to determine where a distribution center should be located so that the total number of miles driven is minimized.

As students make guesses as to where the distribution center should be located, they must find the distances to each of the five restaurants. For example, suppose students guess that the distribution center should be located at mile marker 20. To find the distance to the restaurants, they should experience a small disequilibrium, as they subtract $20 - 2$, $20 - 4$, and $20 - 16$ to find the distances to the first three restaurants, but then need to switch the order, subtracting $28 - 20$ and $50 - 20$. Why can they not be consistent in the order of subtraction? This leads to the need for and the idea of absolute value, where we do not care about the direction, but only the distance. With a few similar examples, you can actually lead students to the more formal definition cited above, where the idea is the end result, not the beginning point. Again, problems in the back of the section on absolute value may give you other contexts that can help students develop this intuitive understanding, which is important to achieve before the idea is formalized.

In other words, many math books are written backwards. Rather than starting with the main ideas, try to guide the students so that they develop the ideas for themselves. While skill automation can be desirable and in many cases necessary, it should follow, not lead conceptual understanding. Beginning with the abstractions does not follow our natural sequences of learning and can even reduce the depth of learning[11-13]. Consequently, we encourage you to rearrange the text so that understanding precedes memorization and attempts at skill automation. The text can still be valuable, but know that it's up to you how you use it. After all, you, not the text, are in control of the curriculum.

In science, the solution is often a bit different. Instead of providing prescriptive labs, think about ways that students can engage in the science related to the concept. This often means trying to allow some flexibility in one or more of the following: stating the problem or question, defining the procedure to study the problem, collecting and organizing the data, analyzing the data, and communicating ideas. Students are often able to write their own procedure for a lab, but when allowing them to do this, it is important that you sign off each procedure before they actually conduct the experiment. This ensures that safety has been checked and the procedure is appropriate. It is true that there are some labs where it is important to provide the procedure ahead of time. For instance, students should not discover how to conduct a titration in chemistry or perform a gel electrophoresis in biology. However, the point should be clear that we tend to give students far too much information, which results in inhibiting their thinking. Finally, explanation of material is important, but we do not need a lecture on photosynthesis before students begin exploring how plants get their energy and food and what they respire as a byproduct. Let us put it another way:

have you ever had a student that comes to class excited to learn about mitosis or limiting reagents? Those are important ideas, but they should be ideas that arise from an investigation in which students see a need to learn them, rather than our providing the information and then trying to convince them how important it is.

Fear of Failure

In addition to fear of change, fear of failure is one of the roadblocks we have encountered as teachers move toward a more inquiry-based approach. Perhaps we fear that our students will discover that we are flawed human beings who don't have all of the answers. Perhaps we fear that, once we start allowing some noise and movement in the classroom, we will never be able to rein in the students again. Perhaps we fear that we will fall in the eyes of administrators who do not understand inquiry-based instruction. Or perhaps we simply fear that we do not have enough experience and knowledge to make this change successful.

These fears are natural and, unless they prevent you from moving in a desired direction, not all bad. They can make you more reflective and your teaching more intentional. We hope that this book, along with your other professional development experiences, helps you overcome the fears that hold you back and provides you with the evidence to convince you of the merits of inquiry-based practice. Nevertheless, we know the fears are real.

Certainly we need to earn the respect of our students, but we can do so by showing respect for them and their ideas, something that is often lacking in a traditional setting. If students see that we don't have all of the answers and even make some mistakes, they often gain confidence by recognizing that it is okay not to know something, resulting in a greater willingness to tackle new ideas.

Managing students' behavior, as discussed in Chapter 6, is certainly different in an inquiry-based classroom, but by having the respect of the students, we can still provide structure while we simultaneously give them greater control over their own learning. Convincing administrators that we know what we are doing can also be achieved. Certainly we need to have established a relationship of mutual trust and respect; without this relationship, anything we do can be challenged. However, if we have built a relationship and our instruction is intentional, with decisions based on evidence, we can provide whatever support might be needed to convince the administrators that our practice is sound. We have to be professionals, with the confidence that comes from knowing that we are the ones who have studied the content and the pedagogy essential for effective instruction. In regard to a lack of experience, you can start small and build incrementally toward a practice that is more inquiry-based. If you currently do not use any inquiry, perhaps set aside one period every other week to begin trying it. Establish a plan so that over a period of several months, maybe even more than a year, you will reach your goal of what you perceive to be the ideal percent of time spent using inquiry-based practices.

We all have fears of the unknown and fears that we will let our students, our administrators, and ourselves down. However, if we recognize that we can do better, we simply need to try to do so. Having others to work with as we make these changes, something discussed earlier, can make a world of difference in facing up to the challenges a paradigm shift presents. But no matter the circumstances, as professionals, each one of us needs to do what we believe is best for our students.

The J-Curve Effect

As we mentioned earlier in this book, sometimes significant change is accompanied by what is called the J-Curve effect. Most people will not see the major leaps that Cathy's students took during their initial inquiry-based experiences. In fact, we might initially see a small dip in student achievement before we see significant gains, much as the shape of the letter *J* suggests. Cathy's students did not experience this for several reasons: 1) their achievement had already bottomed out; 2) Cathy was fully vested in inquiry-based practice; 3) the administration was fully behind Cathy's change in practice and had been grasping for something different to do with their at-risk students; and 4) we had a team working together with this one class. Chances are you won't have all of these working for you, so positive results may take a little more time.

A dip in results can be quite daunting. In fact, many innovations that have the potential to be successful are often abandoned before they have been given sufficient time for growth to occur. Change always carries with it unforeseen challenges that make shifting our instructional practice more difficult than first assumed. As you adjust to new strategies, the students will also adjust, but things are unlikely to change immediately.

Certainly you will be disappointed if you see an initial decrease in student achievement. Recognize that this is common and not an indication that inquiry-based instruction does not work. If you believe that inquiry-based strategies promote deeper understanding and better critical thinking, then stay the course. Be positive and continue to learn and strive to improve your practice. Work with and seek the help of others. This is another reason why we recommend incremental change rather than trying to change everything at once. The evidence is strong that inquiry-based practice will work with all of your students; give it, and yourself, time. For those that see immediate positive results, realize that the improvements will likely become even more dramatic over time.

SUMMARY

In this chapter, we have suggested a strategy for improving your practice over time and have pointed out some of the challenges that you might incur as you transform to an inquiry-based practice. If you come across an obstacle that we have not discussed, contact us, your peers, or other professionals and begin brainstorming a viable solution. One thing we are convinced of, from our personal experiences in research and in teaching, and from our reading of the research that others have done, is that inquiry-based instruction is far more effective than traditional strategies in helping students learn to think critically, solve problems, and learn content at deeper levels.

ENDNOTES

1.   Dewey, J., *How we think*. D.C. Heath: Lexington, Mass, 1910.

2.   Dewey, J., *Experience and education*. Collier Books: New York, 1938.

3.   Chval, K.; Abell, S. K.; Pareja, E.; Musikul, K.; Rizka, G., Science and mathematics teachers' experiences, needs, and expectations regarding professional development. *Eurasia Journal of Mathematics, Science & Technology Education* 2008, 4, (1), 31-43.

4.   Fraser, C.; Kennedy, A.; Reid, L.; McKinney, S., Teachers' continuing professional development: Contested concepts, understandings and models. *Journal of In-Service Education* 2007, 33, (2), 153-169.

5.   Loucks-Horsley, S.; Love, N.; Stiles, K. E.; Mundry, S.; Hewson, P. W., *Designing professional development for teachers of science and mathematics*. Corwin Press, Inc.: Thousand Oaks, CA, 2003.

6.   Cobb, P.; Wood, T.; Yackel, E., Classrooms as learning environments for teachers and researchers. In *Constructivist Views of the Teaching and Learning of Mathematics*, Davis, R. B.; Maher, C. A.; Noddings, N., Eds. NCTM: Reston, VA, 1990; pp 125-146.

7.   Bybee, R. W.; Taylor, J. A.; Gardner, A.; Scotter, P. V.; Powell, J. C.; Westbrook, A.; Landes, N. *The BSCS 5E instructional model: Origins, effectiveness, and applications*; BSCS: Colorado Springs, June-July, 2006; p 49.

8.   Marshall, J. C.; Horton, B.; Smart, J., 4E x 2 Instructional Model: Uniting three learning constructs to improve praxis in science and mathematics classrooms. *Journal of Science Teacher Education* In Press.

9.   Thompson, A., Teachers' beliefs and conceptions: A synthesis of the research. In *Handbook of research on mathematics teaching and learning: A project of the National Council of Teachers of Mathematics*, Grouws, D. A., Ed. MacMillan: NY, 1992; pp 127-146.

10.   Conney, T. J., A beginning teacher's view of problem solving. *Journal for Research in Mathematics Education* 1985, 16, (5), 324-336.

11.   Brownell, W. A., The revolution in arithmetic. *Arithmetic Teacher* 1986, March, 38-42.

12.   Bruner, J. S., *Toward a theory of instruction*. Belkapp Press: Cambridge, 1966.

13.   Jensen, E., *Teaching with the brain in mind*. ASCD: Alexandra, VA, 1998.

CHAPTER 8

SUGGESTIONS FOR EDUCATIONAL LEADERS

Now that your school or district has committed to inquiry-based instruction, what can you do to ensure that the transformation runs as smoothly as possible, that it is not derailed? Many well-intended innovations fail. Leadership is fundamental to the success of any worthy instructional innovation and this includes inquiry-based instruction. Remembering that leadership is not a position, but the responsibility of many when it comes to developing, implementing, and sustaining instructional improvement, leadership for inquiry must come from multiple groups—involving both formal and informal school leaders.

First, leadership must come from credible teacher leaders who possess skills to advocate for inquiry-based instruction and can model for others while they also hone their own instructional skills in inquiry. These teacher leaders then step beyond their sphere of classroom influence to marshal support from fellow teachers, school and district instructional support personnel, and the school principal. Teacher leaders are the content and instructional experts and serve as conduits to the principal to identify resource and training needs so inquiry-based instruction can succeed. Teacher leaders help keep track of the "pulse" or health of the inquiry efforts, communicate with other leaders, and request additional support as it is needed. Teacher leaders are on the front lines in the effort since they see issues first-hand on a daily basis.

Likewise, principals have a tremendous role for advocating for inquiry-based instruction both inside and outside their schools. They must provide emotional and moral support and the resources that are essential for transformation to occur, including teacher time, instructional materials, and classroom equipment essential to effective instruction. Just as important, principals must provide opportunities for job-embedded support and feedback for teachers as they incorporate inquiry into practice. Extensive teacher training that occurs during summer months or after-school hours cannot by itself ensure that teacher learning transfers into classroom practice. As a result, principals have to make sure there is a system in place to support teacher learning and growth in inquiry instruction over time, recognizing that teachers start with different skill sets and levels of understanding. They also need a reasonable understanding of inquiry-based concepts themselves if they are to provide appropriate and useful teacher feedback during classroom visits. Finally, principals must know how to tap both internal and external support resources to help teachers as they progress from novice to proficient in their use of inquiry methods.

Effective adoption and implementation of inquiry instruction also depends on how formal and informal leaders communicate about the efforts. Even the best-laid plans can be quickly shattered by one highly persuasive dissenting voice. Unfortunately, one or two incorrectly informed persons can draw others to their antagonistic cause if proper action is not taken. As with most challenges, doing your homework and clearly communicating with all the stakeholders early in the effort can contribute greatly to eliminating, or at least reducing, this problem. The communication needs to state concisely the goals and expected outcomes, but it must also provide a well-justified argument for the needed change. Such proactive actions provide one method to rein in dissension before it has a chance to develop. Even if total consensus is not possible, and it rarely is, leaders should create opportunities to convey the purpose and evidence for the initiative so that it has a chance to be discussed, developed, and implemented to its maximum potential. When teacher engagement and ownership of the changes have been achieved through clear well-justified communication, positive discourse can be held about the nuances of implementation instead of negative battles that deal with misinformation, opposing viewpoints, and raging factions[1]. The goal is to build an engaged team of participants within the school where fear is reduced and best solutions are sought[2].

Leaders also keep in mind that the parent community must also be informed. Well-meaning parents can hinder and derail progress when they don't understand the reasons for instructional innovations that may be outside their own school experiences. Having the principal and teachers on the same page and speaking the same language about inquiry-based practices is key in parent understanding and support. Effective communication is the best defense for naysayers.

INQUIRY

To communicate effectively, leaders must understand inquiry. So what is inquiry, and just as importantly, what is it not? Though we hope that you read this entire book to gain a deeper understanding, we provide a short summary here. There is considerable confusion surrounding inquiry—partially because of the broad and inconsistent use of the term in education. We have adopted a commonly used and well-respected definition of inquiry:

Inquiry-based instruction is the development of understanding through investigation, i.e., asking questions, determining appropriate methods, gathering data, thinking critically about relationships between evidence and explanations, and formulating and communicating logical arguments—adapted from the National Science Education Standards, 1996, p. 105).

Our expectation is that, with inquiry-based instruction, students become more involved in their own learning, learn at deeper levels, and are more likely to become self-directed, life-long learners. This expectation is grounded in decades of research that suggests that meaningful learning experiences are developed by perturbing one's thinking, linking learning to prior knowledge, and integrating new findings with prior conceptions[3-6]. Whenever possible, students formulate meaningful scientific questions, collect data, analyze the data, communicate their results, and engage in various other facets of the scientific process. The teacher, rather than being the dispenser of knowledge and the teller of facts, helps facilitate and scaffold these investigations by asking essential questions.

For example, to initiate a unit on nutrition, the teacher might ask, "It has been said that you are what you eat. Do you agree with this statement?" To begin, students could explore what they know about the foods they eat and how their bodies interact with these foods. With the teacher's guidance, they will ultimately learn to convey an understanding of the various food groups, how various foods help to fuel and sustain their bodies, and how diet influences their bodies. Inquiry-based instruction contrasts with the transmission of knowledge method of instruction, which assumes that students either have had the same prior experiences or that these experiences do not matter. Further, proponents of traditional methods often assume that most learning occurs because the teacher defines key terms and tells students exactly what they should know.

Non-inquiry methods do still play a role. They are most effective when students are expected to memorize facts and perform and automate calculations and procedures. However, when the objectives entail analyzing, interpreting, predicting, and other deeper cognitive levels, inquiry-based instruction has been shown to be more effective[7].

Myths

A great deal of confusion and misinformation exists regarding inquiry-based instruction. Below are several commonly heard myths or misconceptions regarding inquiry-based instruction along with discussion regarding why the statements are false. As a leader, you can use this discussion as you try to prevent that dissenting voice from derailing the transformation to inquiry-based practice in your math and science departments. Remember that concerned parents, ill-informed leaders, or teachers struggling to understand the need for inquiry practice are all possible derailers. The successful leader listens for concerns and various misunderstandings and responds convincingly.

1) Inquiry is an educational free-for-all where kids are turned loose to learn what they want.

FALSE. As with anything, there are extremes, but few if any educational experts that advocate for inquiry instruction recommend just letting kids roam free in their learning. The role of the teacher in inquiry-based instruction, however, does shift from being a lecturer and didactic guru to one of facilitator. The inquiry-based teacher actively questions and challenges; she is actively engaged in conversations—not just Q & A sessions; and she monitors where individual, group, and whole-class input is needed. For instance, if all students seem to be wrestling with the same question, then it is appropriate for the teacher to lead a whole-class discussion to clarify and guide them before they return to their groups to work.

2) Inquiry means that the teacher is not supposed to provide explanations.

FALSE. Being a facilitator means knowing when to listen, when to question, and when to input your ideas. Though students should contribute to explanations whenever possible, it is very appropriate as part of the lesson debriefing for teachers to provide a synthesis or summary to pull all the pieces back together. The key facet of inquiry-based instruction is that students are required to think, not just absorb what the teacher is saying.

3) Providing activities for students or keeping students busy is the same thing as inquiry.

FALSE. Inquiry is much more than just getting students "active" in their learning. Students have to be involved in designing, collecting, analyzing, and communicating their ideas. Many feel that as long as students are busy then learning is taking place. This thinking supports the notion that any activity that relates to the concept being studied is just as good as any other. The result is an activity-mania that plagues many classrooms where students are busy, but the level of thinking is shallow. Initially, it may be difficult to discern the difference between one class working on an activity and another class engaged in an inquiry investigation. But, if you pause to listen to the discussions and classroom interactions, the differences will soon be clear. In the inquiry class, students are asking process type questions—How can we...? How many trials should we conduct? What do our results show us? In the activity-laden class, conversations are about completion and answers—What did you get for #3? Let me see what your graph looks like. What are we supposed to do?

4) Inquiry is not appropriate for all ability levels.

FALSE. In fact, inquiry provides one of the best means to differentiate instruction for all students. Further, when inquiry becomes a substantial and integral portion of classroom instruction, it reduces the need to track students. Specifically, the depth and quality of analysis and communication of ideas that is achieved can vary depending on the ability level of the student, though an overall understanding of the underlying concept and process should be essential for all.

5) To be effective, inquiry should be the sole source of instruction.

FALSE. Variety is critical for high-quality instruction. Inquiry investigations are appropriate for lessons that involve major ideas, connect to other concepts, or require deep cognitive levels. Inquiry experiences provide a nice reference point to reflect back on as learning progresses during the year because students will remember these experiences. Inquiry is not the best option when students are automating skills or algorithms, or the concepts are simple and straightforward. The percent of time that should be devoted to inquiry-based instruction is not etched in stone. However, the results discussed in Chapter 1 indicate that math and science teachers believe that the target should be approximately 50% of the time. We suggest closer to 65% of the time, but if teachers were implementing effective high-quality inquiry experiences at least 50% of the time, learning would be astounding and dramatic for all students.

6) Students are not learning content when they learn through inquiry.

FALSE. This, of course, can be true if inquiry is poorly implemented, or if the teacher equates mere activities with inquiry. Solid inquiry experiences should tie learning with major concepts. For instance, forces and motion is a major unit of study in science that aligns well with inquiry. As students explore forces and motion via data collection, data analysis, and communication of ideas, they are afforded a great opportunity to think deeply and critically about significant concepts instead of just defining the terms, seeing an example, and performing a calculation or two. In mathematics, by exploring population growth over time, students can gain insight into exponential functions that allow them to make predictions and understand why there is such concern over seemingly small outbreaks such as the swine flu. With inquiry, students are able to see concepts in a meaningful context and link them to their prior knowledge and experience.

7) Teachers don't have time to teach all the standards if they use inquiry.

FALSE. It is true that inquiry forms of learning take more time. In fact, learning takes time— period. Consequently, if we do not allow sufficient time, it is often at the expense of achieving enduring understanding. Inquiry may require teachers to prioritize more and even change the units of instruction somewhat, but if inquiry is inextricably linked with the key concepts within the discipline, then time is freed to allow inquiry to become a major instructional strategy. Specifically what would be different? Almost every K-12 science class spends the first part of the year teaching the Scientific Method and ways of knowing in science. There is no reason why this should be taught in isolation of key content. Just because it is Standard 1 for each year does not mean that it should be taught exclusively until it is completed before moving on to Standard 2. When inquiry is well integrated with content, ideas such as independent and dependent variables now have context and meaning when studying motion or factors that influence plant growth. This can easily free up 1-2 weeks each year to allow for integrated inquiry and content. In math, consider how much time is spent reviewing the previous year's work. With inquiry, these ideas can readily be embedded within the current lessons. Furthermore, with inquiry, students remember better because they have a deeper understanding of the material and more neural pathways to their knowledge, so less time is needed revisiting previous topics.

8) Inquiry instruction is counter to effective classroom management techniques.

FALSE. For some, effective classroom management involves having students sit quietly as knowledge is imparted to them. This models compliance, not effective management or effective learning that engages students. Solid management should involve having students actively engaged in a respectful, highly functioning classroom. Yes, there is more noise and more movement in the class, but this noise and movement are purposeful. The teacher must, of course, monitor the behavior and deal firmly with any violations of the rules. In addition, the teacher must help students work well with others, something that becomes much easier as the year progresses and as more and more teachers adopt an inquiry-based approach. Some students (and adults) do not naturally desire to work in groups. However, not working well with others is one of the primary reasons that people are fired from their jobs. So, we can run from this reality, or realize that developing interpersonal abilities is a critical part of what we are responsible to do as teachers and leaders, and know that while we are doing so, we are also helping the students learn at deeper levels of understanding.

IMPORTANT LITERATURE

Too often our decisions are based on how persuasive someone is, regardless of the facts and research behind the initiative. With inquiry, we may need to do just the opposite and work on our persuasive skills, or at least communication skills, because the research to support inquiry instruction in math and science is clear and abundant. Here are some of the realities regarding inquiry-based instruction.

1) Science and Mathematics Standards Emphasize Inquiry

By far, the two most important guides for science and math standards in the U.S. are the *National Science Education Standards*[8] (*NSES*) and the *Principles and Standards for School Mathematics*[9] (*PSSM*). These two guides form the foundation for state standards throughout the U.S. The *NSES* unequivocally states that we need to emphasize inquiry instruction to a greater extent while emphasizing transmission of knowledge to a lesser extent. In science, one of the eight big national standards is inquiry, and nature of science, which is closely related, is another. In math, five of the ten total standards are process standards that emphasize aspects such as problem solving and representation. This alone should make the point clear that inquiry must be brought into every classroom for every child in a meaningful way.

The manner that individual state standards address inquiry in math and in science varies, but in South Carolina, which we believe is representative of many states in this regard, it has a clear focus. In science at every grade level, the first of 4-6 total standards each year is inquiry. In mathematics, every grade level and high school core area begins with the five process standards identified by NCTM. That means that teachers should, without question, be leading inquiry instruction in both math and science. However, many do not see that this inquiry can and should be integrated with the content being studied and not separated from it. Further, many of the state tests now emphasize content and process, which means that students now have to be able to interpret graphs or scenarios instead of just calculating or defining. Our approach is to view the process standards as both an end and a means to another end. As an end, we want every student to become proficient in the scientific processes that inquiry entails. As a means, we should be using the process standards as the primary strategy for helping our students master the key content standards. In this way, process and content are fully integrated.

2) Large-Scale Initiatives Support Inquiry-Based Instruction

There is much more information that supports the reform toward greater amounts of inquiry instruction. First, all teachers who go through National Board Teacher Certification[10,11] are required to demonstrate competency in inquiry-based instruction. Second, *Understanding by Design*[12] has been adopted by scores of teachers, departments, and districts throughout the nation. Its premise is to focus on identifying and then leading instruction that centers on enduring ideas. This aligns beautifully with inquiry, which promotes the deep understanding of critical or enduring ideas. Further, inquiry is complementary to other initiatives such as Learning-Focused[13]. Inquiry furthers the work of Learning-Focused by enhancing activities with intentional investigations that are designed to encourage deep and critical thinking; quite simply, the framework of Learning-Focused is supportive of inquiry-based instruction, not counter to it.

3) National Assessments and Labor Force Reports Indicate Students Lack Inquiry Skills

Additionally, national and international tests, such as the NAEP[14], TIMMS[15,16], and PISA[17], continue to show that Americans are missing the mark when it comes to critical thinking skills in math and science education. Finally, numerous commissions have reported that it is a moral imperative and essential for success in tomorrow's workforce that our students become deep thinkers who can critically examine ideas and communicate in effective ways[18,19].

An entire body of research on change and the role of leaders has been conducted over the past decades. It is not our purpose here to delve deeply into this research, but for those who wish to do so, you may be especially interested in the work of Hord and Fullan, who have investigated stages of concern and levels of change (adoption, implementation, and institutionalization, respectively.

GETTING PARENTS AND COMMUNITY RESOURCES ON YOUR SIDE

One of the greatest challenges is getting parents to see that the needs of today's students are very different from when they went through school. There is a belief by many that if it was good enough for them, then it should be good enough for their kids. This belief only perpetuates thinking that change is not needed because, after all, if it isn't broken then we shouldn't fix it. Well, it is broken, and the needs are indeed different today. The new job market has a great demand for people who are knowledgeable in science, technology, engineering, and mathematics. Thus, content is critical, but a recent conference held with many technology and engineering companies made it clear that graduates typically come to business and industry with sufficient content knowledge, but they are lacking in creativity, problem-solving, and teamwork that is necessary in tackling new challenges in today's global markets[20]. These are concerns that an inquiry-based approach addresses directly.

What also needs to be clear to parents is that inquiry is a strategy that promotes higher order thinking skills[7]. When inquiry is used as a regular part of instruction, students' ability to reason and solve problems increases. Yes, it may be different than how they learned, but inquiry instruction helps facilitate learning that will be competitive in a global economy. Communication to gain widespread support is especially important here, and we encourage you as leaders to take advantage of the many opportunities that arise. For example, when you prepare school report card narratives to parents to explain goals and initiatives; craft school brochures, newsletters, or school websites to highlight initiatives; make presentations to parents about your academic and instructional goals; network with business and industry through civic organizations to address how you are responding to the needs of the workforce; host parent-classroom visitation days; sponsor math and science learning nights for parent—all of these are opportunities to spread and co-create the vision for more inquiry-based practices.

LEVELS OF SUPPORT

Clear, Supportive Message

Leaders can, in numerous ways, support the development of inquiry-based practice and encourage the sustained efforts once it has been developed. First, your message must be consistent and clear. You must be able to:

1) Concisely articulate the call for reform efforts that focus on inquiry-based instruction,

2) Clearly distinguish how inquiry is different from non-inquiry forms of teaching, and

3) Consistently support teachers, department chairs, and curriculum leaders as they begin transitioning toward greater emphasis on inquiry instruction.

How do teachers know that your support for inquiry-based instruction goes beyond mere rhetoric? It becomes a priority in meetings, it is linked to other major initiatives, professional development funding is directed toward supporting the transition toward inquiry practice, conference travel is targeted toward work and learning related to inquiry instruction and learning, it becomes clear that this is a long-term commitment, and time is made to help support the transition. The last item is critical. We cannot be told to do more and more without some tradeoffs[1]. If teachers are being asked to teach differently, then they must have time to do so. What can teachers do less of, or where can time be made to allow them to focus on improving their teaching and learning? Finally, teachers need to see that this is a long-term commitment. Initiatives are a dime-a-dozen, but why is a change to inquiry better than the previous innovations which have come and gone? Specifically, how do they know that there will be staying power with this push? Your commitment, consistency, and dedication can be shown in many ways.

Build a Learning Cohort to Support Inquiry-Based Instruction

When possible, form a cohort of teachers that can work together to change instruction. If funding is limited, as it often is, then try targeting one discipline per year or one grade level per year so that a group of teachers can work through an intensive year of professional development as a group. Set clear goals and expectations as a group that will be targeted during the year. This should be collaborative, but the expectations should be clear that reform is needed. Then, ask the teachers how they believe they can best achieve it. Many schools are organizing themselves into professional learning communities. A group that takes on the study and implementation of inquiry practices can quickly ratchet up teacher knowledge and the status of inquiry practices in the school. Dissemination and fine-tuning rests not only with the school leader or early-adopter teacher, but rests with a team—building ownership and efficacy when teachers study a problem together and work towards its end—in a sense modeling the approach to inquiry that we promote with students.

With a learning cohort, principals can also make good use of an instructional coach or assistant principal to build and improve that individual's leadership skills and knowledge. By serving on a learning cohort with teachers, they can get first-hand experience in supporting teachers on implementation issues related to inquiry instruction. Learning cohorts can be powerful in helping to build the leadership capacity needed to institutionalize inquiry-based instruction beyond a small group of teachers.

Take Time to Celebrate Success

From time to time, it is important to celebrate and acknowledge success. Not all teachers are going to be extraordinary (by definition), but all teachers can and should be on a track to improve performance to at least a level deemed proficient. Part of the celebration could include having each teacher share one thing that she has tried with inquiry instruction that has led to improved learning. This could range from a rubric to a creative idea to a management technique to a new way to explain concepts after students have had time to explore. Strong principals make effective use of faculty meeting time—keeping business details to a minimum and targeting aspects of professional practice at every meeting. You might consider using 15-20 minutes at each faculty or departmental meeting to have teachers share techniques, having roundtable discussions about challenges they face, or reading and reflecting on an article about inquiry; in all of these ways you are bringing educator development to the forefront. What leaders spend their time on—and teachers' time on in faculty meetings—is a powerful way to communicate what is valued in the school. If inquiry instruction is important, leaders will increase its visibility in professional dialogue. These actions do much to validate and recognize teacher hard work in inquiry-based instruction.

Sustained Practice

It is important to keep things going after positive change has been made. Conversations with teachers may help to determine how to sustain the change and support further growth. One of the challenges with any initiative is that we too often stop before we really know whether it works. We typically do not perform at our best when we try something only once. To make the point, new teachers typically are not at their best until many years into teaching. The J-curve phenomenon suggests that as a new reform is implemented that a lag, and even a slight drop, may occur initially[21]. If the reform is effective, student outcomes will improve in the long run, provided that sufficient time is allowed[22]. We need to base our decisions on the best research and evidence that we have for what entails good instruction and learning. Then, we need to allow sufficient time to allow it to be implemented and refined to see how it really works.

CLASSROOM MANAGEMENT ISSUES

As we have discussed, one of the greatest impediments that may be standing in the way of teachers succeeding with inquiry is their ability to manage their classroom effectively. It would be easy to cast aside efforts to improve inquiry-based instruction because of management challenges, but a better solution is to address the management issues directly. If management is a challenge, and it often is—particularly since there is more fear surrounding classroom management than any other issue—then focus on the key issues and work through them as a cohort. Further, individual teachers can be supported in solving issues that are not globally shared. Highly structured teachers may struggle with student management as they move from less teacher-directed methods to more teacher-facilitated methods. Teachers who resist inquiry may do so because they lack confidence and fear they may lose control of students. Teachers will not step out unless they know they will be supported and can feel confident that when they are learning new skills, they are not expected to be at a masterful level of implementation right away. School leaders bear the responsibility to create risk-free or at least risk-tolerant environments so teachers can develop. School leaders need to talk with teachers about the differences between formative and summative evaluations and the importance of feedback—removing the "gotcha mentality" and instilling instead the continuous growth mentality for teachers as they adopt inquiry-based instruction. When a teacher is in the process of learning and experimenting with inquiry, formative and risk-free feedback is essential.

The solution should start with the most critical items first—focusing on only one or two issues at a time. For instance, teachers often have to readjust their paradigm to understand that student compliance and silence do not equate to learning. So, conversations can be held that focus on what interactions look like in an inquiry environment. It is important that school leaders are part of these discussions so that they can convey what they expect to see when they observe classes.

So where can time be found to have such discussions? First, many schools have a faculty meeting once a week. Business items that could easily be conveyed via a weekly email often consume these meetings. Another option is for teams to meet if there are common planning times. The goal is to address the challenges head-on instead of avoiding them. Every effort should be made to provide the support necessary to attain the goal—effective management that allows inquiry-based instruction. Finally, if setting up face-to-face meetings to confront issues presents too many challenges, then begin a school blog for teachers. The blog could have key issues that have been identified and give teachers a medium to support each other through the discussion threads. This is an opportunity for teachers to take leadership roles with their peers. When roadblocks seem to be reached that the teachers are not able to solve, then consider bringing in an expert to help facilitate the solutions with the issue at hand. Chapter 6 provides a more detailed discussion about effective management issues if more specific information is desired.

ASSESSING AND EVALUATING INQUIRY

Chapters 4 and 5 focus on assessing teacher performance related to inquiry instruction and assessing student achievement. Below we provide a brief summary of these issues along with other evaluation issues that face teachers and other educational leaders.

EQUIP

First of all, what does successful inquiry look like, and what are some key things that should be targeted from an administrator's standpoint? The Appendix provides the Electronic Quality of Inquiry Protocol (EQUIP)) that is intended to be used by teachers, researchers, and school leaders. The first several sections of EQUIP are directed more toward researchers. In sections IV-VIII, a descriptive rubric is provided to guide the assessment of the quality of inquiry that is being facilitated in the classroom. The rubric was designed so that Level 3 is considered proficient for each of the 19 indicators. While there is significant importance to each of the indicators, looking at 19 different aspects at one time and then targeting progress for each of these is overwhelming. Thus, we recommend that specific indicators be targeted for a given observation. Targeted indicators can be identified by the teacher, department, or school administration, depending on the type of conversations that you intend to have.

Two key indicators that you might wish to begin focusing conversations and observations on are *Order of Instruction* and *Classroom Interactions*. Proficient *Order of Instruction* requires that teachers provide ways for students to explore ideas before formal explanations occur and that students are involved in the explanation. This indicator often leads to some heated discussions, but the research is clear that we must engage the learner in the content before providing explanations if we want deep conceptual understanding to occur. Those who question whether this can be done in the classroom are really asking for help and guidance because they have not seen it or know how to lead it. This is where bringing in consultants or curriculum specialists can be extremely helpful. Regardless of who is brought in to help, the interactions need to be very pragmatic for the teachers. These interactions can range from observing a specialist model a lesson to co-teaching to discussing and brainstorming together about a videotaped lesson.

The second indicator, *Classroom Interactions*, speaks to the quality of discourse that occurs in the classroom. Are we asking lower-level questions, or are we facilitating discussions that challenge students to think at deeper levels? And, yes, this indicator is meant for all ability levels of students.

EQUIP is not the only means to assess or guide discussions among teachers, but it is a solid, reliable, and valid measure that can help guide the development in clear and specific ways. Even if the intention is not to use EQUIP as a formal instrument, it may help administrators as they make informal classroom visits to better understand what is transpiring in the classroom. One caveat is in order: EQUIP is not designed as a tool to evaluate overall teacher performance. It focuses on inquiry instruction; on lessons that target objectives for which inquiry is not the best strategy, typically those that require memorization, automation of procedures, or low-level cognition, the ratings will necessarily be low. Consequently, it is critical that the evaluator understand the purpose of the observed lesson.

Finally, new teachers are held to a set of standards that measure their competence in their first years of teaching. The standards vary from state to state, but most have been derived from the INTASC (Interstate New Teacher Assessment and Support Consortium) Standards. Inquiry flows seamlessly into the teaching portfolios and competencies that INTASC requires. For instance, the importance of inquiry can and should appear in places such as the teaching philosophy statement, the classroom management plan, the long and short-term planning, instructional strategies used, and assessment of learning. Instructional leaders can look for these and discuss these explicitly with each of their new teachers.

In the end, for inquiry-based reform efforts to succeed, several key issues need to be addressed. These include: 1) developing and communicating a clear, evidence-based vision, 2) engaging faculty in the adoption of and then the implementation of the initiative, 3) providing long-term commitment and support, 4) finding ways to free up time instead of just asking for more from teachers, 5) assisting in creating effectively managed classrooms, and 6) developing improvement plans using instruments such as EQUIP. The need for reform is clear. Yes, change can be challenging, but the success can be truly amazing when teams and schools work collectively to improve teaching and learning.

ENDNOTES

1.   Reeves, D. B., *Leading change in your school: How to conquer myths, build commitment, and get results*. ASCD: Alexandria, VA, 2009.

2.   Deutschman, A., *Change or die: The three keys to change at work and in life*. Harper Collins: New York, NY, 2007.

3.   Bransford, J. D.; Brown, A. L.; Cocking, R. R., *How people learn: Brain, mind, experience, and school (expanded edition)*. National Academies Press: Washington, DC, 2000.

4.   Jensen, E., *Teaching with the brain in mind*. ASCD: Alexandra, VA, 1998.

5.   Piaget, J., Piaget's theory. In *Carmichael's manual of child psychology*, Mussen, P. H., Ed. Wiley: New York, 1970; pp 703-32.

6.   Vygotsky, L., *Mind in society: The development of higher psychological processes*. Harvard University Press: Cambridge, 1978.

7.   Marshall, J. C.; Horton, R. M., The relationship of teacher facilitated inquiry-based instruction to student higher-order thinking. *School Science and Mathematics* In Review.

8.   National Research Council, *National science education standards*. National Academies Press: Washington, DC, 1996.

9.   National Council of Teachers of Mathematics, *Principles and standards for school mathematics*. NCTM, Inc.: Reston, VA, 2000.

10.   National Board for Professional Teaching Standards, *What teachers should know and be able to do*. Author: Washington, DC, 1994.

11.   National Board for Professional Teaching Standards *A distinction that matters: Why national teacher certification makes a difference*; Center for Educational Research and Evaluation: Greensboro, NC, 2000.

12.   Wiggins, G.; McTighe, J., *Understanding by design*. ASCD: Alexandria, VA, 1998.

13.   Thompson, M.; Thompson, J., *Learning-Focused strategies notebook*. Learning Concepts: Boone, NC, 2005.

14.   National Assessment of Educational Progress *NAEP 2000 science assessment results released*; NCES 2002-452; United States Department of Education, : Jessup, MD, 2002.

15.   Schmidt, W. H.; McNight, C. C.; Raizen, S. A. A splintered vision: An investigation of U.S. science and mathematics education. http://imc.lisd.k12.mi.us/MSC1/Timms.html

16.   U.S. National Research Center Third international mathematics and science study (TIMSS). http://ustimss.msu.edu/

17.   Baldi, S.; Jin, Y.; Skemer, M.; Green, P. J.; Herget, D. *Highlights from PISA 2006: Performance of U.S. 15-year-old students in science and mathematics literacy in an international context (NCES 2008-016)*; National Center for Education Statistics, Institute of Education Sciences, U.S. Department of Education: Washington, DC, 2007.

18.   National Commission on Mathematics and Science Teaching, *Before its too late: A report to the nation from the National Commission on Mathematics and Science Teaching for the 21st Century*. U.S. Department of Education: Washington, DC, 2000.

19.   National Academy of Sciences, *Rising above the gathering storm: Energizing and employing America for a brighter economic future.* National Academies Press: Washington, DC, 2007.

20.   Friedman, T., *The world is flat: A brief history of the twenty-first century.* Farrar, Straus and Giroux: New York, 2005.

21.   Erb, T. O.; Stevenson, C., Middle school reforms throw a J-Curve: Don't strike out. *Middle School Journal* 1999, 45-47.

22.   Yore, L.; Anderson, J.; Shymansky, J., Sensing the impact of elementary school science reform: A study of stakeholder perceptions of implementation, constructivist strategies, and school-home collaboration. *Journal of Science Teacher Education* 2005, 16, (1), 65-88.

CONCLUSION

J ust as our students need to debrief at the culmination of an inquiry learning experience to make sense of the concepts and ideas, we as educational professionals also need to debrief and reflect on the learning that we have facilitated in our classrooms. You may have caught yourself nodding in agreement as you read many of the ideas shared in this book, or perhaps you found yourself challenging some of the ideas presented. Regardless, we now ask, "So what?" How will any of this influence what you do on a daily basis with your students?

First, we assume that if you got this far that you are motivated to bring inquiry into the classroom. Yes, transforming practice to greater quality and quantity of inquiry comes with its share of challenges, but the potential increase in depth of student performance should warrant a willingness to work through these challenges. You will almost certainly be frustrated in your efforts if you change everything all at once, and your students will be as well. Instead, reflect on your practice, determine one or two areas where you believe you can make a successful change, and then continue on a path of incremental change to move toward your vision of high-quality inquiry instruction.

You know better than anyone what is most likely to work for you, but here are a few areas where we would recommend placing the greatest attention:

1) Make sure students are provided frequent opportunities to explore major concepts *before* formal explanation is provided. For many, this will require a paradigm shift. Instead of thinking, "*I must explain* before they can do it," ask yourself, "*How can I engage* them and have them explore the ideas in a meaningful way before an explanation occurs?"

2) Be intentional about your classroom practices; don't just try to fill up the time. Being intentional means that you reflect almost constantly on why you do what you do and then base your decisions on what is best for the students. Further, it means that you are regularly using formative assessments to direct your decisions regarding the next steps that need to be taken. Your underlying thought should be how to push, encourage, and challenge all students to grow and to learn at deep levels that allow them to transfer their understandings to new situations.

3) Build a cohort of likeminded teachers who are willing to engage in regular conversations regarding instructional practice. Sure, individual teachers can and do make significant differences with their students. However, a powerful synergy is created when several teachers work together to improve the quality of inquiry in their classrooms. The resulting conversations help to keep each of you accountable, provide support when you need it, and build a culture of consistently high expectations for student performance.

4) Get in the habit of listening more to your students and letting their thoughts help guide where the class needs to head next. Certainly you have standards and objectives that you need to address; consequently, you need to set the major direction. Nevertheless, you need to be flexible, without ever losing site of the final destination. Every class is different and every student's needs differ; this is why teachers are needed. By making sure your lessons are tied to "big ideas" in the discipline, you will have more flexibility to veer a little from your lesson plan. Allow students' questions, concerns, and gaps or misconceptions to steer you a little off course so that you are addressing their needs. Ultimately, if they aren't learning, you're not really teaching.

5) Create engaging, meaningful learning opportunities that are tied to real world problems and in some way connect to your students' experience and interests. When you are attuned to the needs and abilities of your students, you are better able to help them excel by providing timely curriculum that ties to their own understanding of the world, energizes them, and motivates them to learn. Not only will students no longer ask, "When will I ever use this?", but they will learn at much deeper levels.

The journey of teaching is an amazing one that has intrinsic rewards far beyond most careers. When students are engaged and challenged, teaching and learning become an exciting, joint venture, one in which you make a significant difference in their lives. There is no magic elixir that guarantees success in the classroom, but we hope that the suggestions we have made and the conversations that you engage in as a result of this book will help to tilt the scales toward successful inquiry-based instruction in your classroom.

APPENDIX
EQUIP
(Electronic Quality of Inquiry Protocol)

Complete Sections I before and during observation, Sections II and III during the observation, and Sections IV-VII immediately after the observation. If a construct in Sections IV-VI absolutely cannot be coded based on the observation, then it is to be left blank.

Observation date: _____ Time start: _____ Time end: _____ Observer: _____

School: _____ District: _____ Teacher: _____ Course: _____

I. Descriptive Information

A. Teacher Descriptive Information:

1. Teacher gender _____ Male (M), Female (F)

2. Teacher ethnicity _____ Caucasian (C), African-American (A), Latino (L), Other (O)

3. Grade level(s) observed _____ 4. Subject/Course observed _____

5. Highest degree _____ 6. Number of years experience: _____ 7. Number of years teaching this content _____

B. Student/Class Descriptive Information

1. Number of students in class:

2. Gender distribution: _____ Males _____ Females

3. Ethnicity distribution _____ Caucasian (C) _____ African-American (A) _____ Latino (L) _____ Other

C. Lesson Descriptive Information

1. Is the lesson an exemplar that follows the 4E x 2 Instructional Model? (PDI exemplar, non-PDI exemplar, non-exemplar)

2. Working title for lesson:

3. Objectives/Purpose of lesson: Inferred (I), Explicit (E) _____:

4. Standards addressed: State (S), District (D), None Explicit (N) _____:

INQUIRY IN
MOTION
www.clemson.edu/iim

EQUIP–2009

II. Time Usage Analysis

Time	Activity Codes	Organization Codes	Student Attention to Lesson Codes	Cognitive Codes	Inquiry Instruction Component Codes	Assessment Codes
0-5						
5-10						
10-15						
15-20						
20-25						
25-30						
30-35						
35-40						
40-45						
45-50						
50-55						
55-60						
60-65						
65-70						
70-75						
75-80						
80-85						

Activity Codes—facilitated by teacher

0. **Non-instructional time**—administrative tasks, handing back/collecting papers, general announcements, time away from instruction
1. **Pre-inquiry**—teacher-centered, passive students, prescriptive, didactic discourse pattern, no inquiry attempted
2. **Developing inquiry**—teacher-centered with some active engagement of students, prescriptive though not entirely, mostly didactic with some open-ended discussions, teacher dominates the explain, teacher seen as both giver of knowledge and as a facilitator, beginning of class warm-ups
3. **Proficient inquiry**—largely student-centered, focus on students as active learners, inquiries are guided and include student input, discourse includes discussions that emphasize process as much as product, teacher facilitates learning and students active in all stages, including the explain phase
4. **Exemplary inquiry**—student-centered, students active in constructing understanding of content, rich teacher-student and student-student dialogue, teacher facilitates learning in effective ways to encourage student learning and conceptual development, assumptions and misconceptions are challenged by students and teacher

Organization Codes—led by teacher

W Whole class
S Small group
I Individual work

Student Attention to Lesson Code—displayed by students

L **Low attention**, 20% or fewer attending to the lesson. Most students are off-task – heads on desks, staring out of the window, chatting with neighbors, etc.
M **Medium attention**, between 20-80% of students are attending to the lesson.
H **High attention**, 80% or more of the students are attending to the lesson. Most students are taking notes or looking at the teacher during lecture, writing on the worksheet, most students are volunteering ideas during a discussion, most students are engaged in small group discussions even without the presence of the teacher.

Cognitive Code—displayed by students

0. Other–e.g. classroom disruption, non-instructional portion of lesson, administrative activity
1. Receipt of knowledge
2. Lower order (recall, remember, understand) and/or activities focused on completion exercises, computation
3. Apply (demonstrate, modify, compare) and/or activities focused on problem solving
4. Analyze/Evaluate (evidence, verify, analyze, justify, interpret)
5. Create (combine, construct, develop, formulate)

Inquiry Instructional Component Code—facilitated by teacher

0. **Non-inquiry**: activities with the purpose of skill automation; rote memorization of facts; drill and practice; checking answers on homework, quizzes, or classwork with little or no explanation
1. **Engage**: typically situated at the beginning of the lesson; assessing student prior knowledge and misconceptions; stimulating student interest
2. **Explore**: students investigate a new idea or concept
3. **Explain**: teacher or students making sense of an idea or concept
   Extend: [Extend is important but is not coded as such because it typically is a new Engage, Explore, or Explain]

Assessment Code—facilitated by teacher

0. No assessment observed
1. **Monitoring** (circulating around the room, probing for understanding, checking student progress, commenting as appropriate)
2. **Formative assessment** (assessing student progress, instruction modified to align with student ability) or **Diagnostic assessment** (checking for prior knowledge, misconceptions, abilities)
3. **Summative assessment** (assessing student learning, evaluative and not informing next instructional step)

INQUIRY IN MOTION
www.clemson.edu/iim

EQUIP–2009

III. Lesson Descriptive Details

Time (mins into class)	Classroom Notes of Observation	Comments

INQUIRY IN MOTION
www.clemson.edu/iim

EQUIP–2009

IV. Instructional Factors

Construct Measured	Pre-Inquiry (Level 1)	Developing Inquiry (2)	Proficient Inquiry (3)	Exemplary Inquiry (4)
I1. Instructional Strategies	Teacher predominantly lectured to cover content.	Teacher **frequently lectured** and/or used demonstrations to explain content. Activities were **verification only**.	Teacher **occasionally lectured, but students were engaged in activities that** helped develop conceptual understanding.	Teacher occasionally lectured, but students were engaged in investigations that **promoted strong conceptual understanding**.
I2. Order of Instruction	Teacher explained concepts. Students either did not explore concepts or did so only after explanation.	Teacher asked **students to explore concept before** receiving **explanation**. Teacher explained.	Teacher asked students to **explore before explanation**. **Teacher and students explained**.	Teacher asked students to explore concept before explanation occurred. Though perhaps prompted by the teacher, **students provided the explanation**.
I3. Teacher Role	Teacher was center of lesson; rarely acted as facilitator.	**Teacher was center of** lesson; occasionally **acted as facilitator**.	Teacher **frequently** acted as facilitator.	Teacher **consistently and effectively** acted as a facilitator.
I4. Student Role	Students were consistently passive as learners (taking notes, practicing on their own).	**Students were active to a small extent** as learners (highly engaged for very brief moments or to a small extent throughout lesson).	**Students were active as learners** (involved in discussions, investigations, or activities, but not consistently and clearly focused).	Students were **consistently and effectively active as learners** (highly engaged at multiple points during lesson and clearly focused on the task).
I5. Knowledge Acquisition	Student learning focused solely on mastery of facts, information, and/or rote processes.	Student learning focused on **mastery of facts** and process skills without much focus on understanding of content.	Student learning required **application of concepts** and process skills in new situations.	Student learning required **depth of understanding** to be demonstrated relating to content and process skills.

V. Discourse Factors

Construct Measured	Pre-Inquiry (Level 1)	Developing Inquiry (2)	Proficient Inquiry (3)	Exemplary Inquiry (4)
D1. Questioning Level	Questioning rarely challenged students above the remembering level.	Questioning rarely challenged students above the **understanding level**.	Questioning challenged students **up to application or analysis levels.**	Questioning challenged students at various levels, **including at the analysis level or higher; level was varied to scaffold learning.**
D2. Complexity of Questions	Questions focused on one correct answer; typically short answer responses.	Questions focused **mostly on one correct answer;** some open response opportunities.	Questions **challenged students to explain, reason, and/or justify.**	Questions required students to explain, reason, and/or justify. **Students were expected to critique others' responses.**
D3. Questioning Ecology	Teacher lectured or engaged students in oral questioning that did not lead to discussion.	Teacher occasionally **attempted to engage students in discussions or** investigations but was not successful.	Teacher **successfully engaged students** in open-ended questions, discussions, and/or investigations.	Teacher **consistently and effectively engaged students** in open-ended questions, discussions, investigations, and/or reflections.
D4. Communication Pattern	Communication was controlled and directed by teacher and followed a didactic pattern.	Communication was **typically controlled and directed by teacher** with occasional input from other students; mostly didactic pattern.	**Communication was often conversational** with some student questions guiding the discussion.	Communication was **consistently conversational with student questions often guiding the discussion.**
D5. Classroom Interactions	Teacher accepted answers, correcting when necessary, but rarely followed-up with further probing.	Teacher or another student **occasionally followed-up student response** with further low-level probe.	Teacher or another student often **followed-up response** with engaging probe that **required student to justify** reasoning or evidence.	Teacher **consistently and effectively facilitated rich classroom dialogue** where evidence, assumptions, and reasoning were challenged by teacher or other students.

www.clemson.edu/iim

VI. Assessment Factors

Construct Measured	Pre-Inquiry (Level 1)	Developing Inquiry (2)	Proficient Inquiry (3)	Exemplary Inquiry (4)
A1. **Prior Knowledge**	Teacher did not assess student prior knowledge.	Teacher **assessed student prior knowledge but did not modify instruction** based on this knowledge.	Teacher assessed student prior knowledge and then **partially modified instruction** based on this knowledge.	Teacher assessed student prior knowledge and then **modified instruction** based on this knowledge.
A2. **Conceptual Development**	Teacher encouraged learning by memorization and repetition.	Teacher encouraged **product- or answer-focused** learning activities that **lacked critical thinking.**	Teacher encouraged **process-focused** learning activities **that required critical thinking.**	Teacher encouraged process-focused learning activities that involved **critical thinking that connected learning with other concepts.**
A3. **Student Reflection**	Teacher did not explicitly encourage students to reflect on their own learning.	Teacher explicitly encouraged students to **reflect on their** learning but only at a minimal **knowledge level.**	Teacher explicitly encouraged students to **reflect on their** learning at an **understanding level.**	Teacher consistently encouraged students to reflect on their learning at multiple times throughout the lesson; **encouraged students to think at higher levels.**
A4. **Assessment Type**	Formal and informal assessments measured only factual, discrete knowledge.	Formal and informal assessments **measured mostly factual, discrete knowledge.**	Formal and informal assessments **used both factual, discrete knowledge and authentic measures.**	Formal and informal assessment methods **consistently and effectively used authentic measures.**
A5. **Role of Assessing**	Teacher solicited predetermined answers from students requiring little explanation or justification.	Teacher **solicited information from students to assess understanding.**	Teacher solicited explanations from students to assess **understanding and then adjusted instruction accordingly.**	Teacher frequently and effectively assessed student understanding and adjusted instruction accordingly; **challenged evidence and claims made; encouraged curiosity and openness.**

VII. Curriculum Factors

	Construct Measured	Pre-Inquiry (Level 1)	Developing Inquiry (2)	Proficient Inquiry (3)	Exemplary Inquiry (4)
C1.	Content Depth	Lesson provided only superficial coverage of content.	Lesson provided **some depth** of content but with **no connections made to the big picture.**	Lesson provided depth of content with **some significant connection** to the big picture.	Lesson provided depth of content with **significant, clear, and explicit connections** made to the big picture.
C2.	Learner Centrality	Lesson did not engage learner in activities or investigations.	Lesson provided **prescribed activities** with anticipated results.	Lesson allowed for **some flexibility during investigation** for student-designed exploration.	Lesson provided **flexibility for students to design and carry out** their own investigations.
C3.	Integration of Content and Investigation	Lesson either content-focused or activity-focused but not both.	Lesson provided poor integration of content with activity or investigation.	Lesson **incorporated student investigation that linked well with content.**	Lesson **seamlessly integrated the content and the student investigation.**
C4.	Organizing & Recording Information	Students organized and recorded information in prescriptive ways.	**Students had only minor input as to how to organize and record information.**	Students regularly organized and recorded information in **non-prescriptive ways.**	Students organized and recorded information in **non-prescriptive** ways that allowed them to **effectively communicate their learning.**

www.clemson.edu/iim

VIII. Summative Overviews*

		Comprehensive Score**
Summative view of Instruction		
Summative view of Discourse		
Summative view of Assessment		
Summative view of Curriculum		
Overall view of Lesson		

*Provide brief descriptive comments to justify score.

**Score for each component should be an integer from 1-4 that corresponds with the appropriate level of inquiry. Scores should reflect the essence of the lesson relative to that component, so they need not be an exact average of all sub-scores in a category.

Marshall, J. C., Horton, B., Smart, J., & Llewellyn, D. (2008). *EQUIP: Electronic Quality of Inquiry Protocol*: Retrieved from Clemson University's Inquiry in Motion Institute, www.clemson.edu/iim.

www.clemson.edu/iim

EQUIP–2009

ABOUT THE AUTHORS

Dr. Jeff Marshall and Dr. Bob Horton serve as Co-Directors for the Inquiry in Motion Institute and the Center of Excellence for Inquiry in Mathematics and Science, which is housed at Clemson University. Individually, Dr. Marshall earned the Presidential Award of Excellence for Mathematics and Science Teaching, is Nationally Board Certified in AYA Science, and continues to research, write, and present work on inquiry teaching and learning in science education. Dr. Horton has received teaching awards at the university, secondary, and corporate levels; was recently named one of the top ten university professors in the nation; and continues to work with teachers and students to improve mathematics teaching and learning. Both Dr. Marshall and Dr. Horton have taught at the middle school and high school levels and now work with both pre-service and in-service teachers at Clemson University.

Made in the USA
Lexington, KY
29 August 2011